THATCHERISM HAYEK

& THE POLITICAL ECONOMICS OF THE CONSERVATIVE PARTY

FLOYD MILLEN

First published in paperback by
Michael Terence Publishing in 2024
www.mtp.agency

Copyright © 2024 Floyd Millen

Floyd Millen has asserted the right to be identified
as the author of this work in accordance with the
Copyright, Designs and Patents Act 1988

ISBN 9781800947580

All rights reserved. No part of this publication may be reproduced,
stored in a retrieval system, or transmitted,
in any form or by any means, electronic, mechanical,
photocopying, recording or otherwise,
without the prior permission of the publisher

Cover design
Copyright © 2024 Michael Terence Publishing

Michael Terence
Publishing

To my parents Edgar and Clova Millen
and to my sons, James, Adam and Myles

CONTENTS

PREFACE 1

INTRODUCTION 3

CHAPTER 1 7
Hayek and his Approach 7
The War, the Nazis and the Fall of European Communism 10
The Collapse of Eastern European Governments 15
    Communism Collapses in Eastern Europe 15
Hayek. An ideological Leap to the Future 21
    Knowledge, Competitive Markets and Price Signals 21

CHAPTER 2 31
One Nation, Churchill and the Conservative Party 31
    Free Trade 35
Post-War Dis-Agreement 46
    Full Employment 48
    Crisis in Confidence 52

CHAPTER 3 61
Enoch Powell, Thatcherism and the New Right 61
A Programme of Change 65
Monetarism & Privatisation 81
Money Supply and a Free Society 107

CHAPTER 4 113
The Perils of Inflation 113
    Labour Unions and Unemployment In a Free Society 118
    Labour Unions and Unemployment 123
    Welfare and a Free Society 129

CHAPTER 5 135
Thatcher's Monetarism: Success or Failure 135
Thatcherism and The Return of (Enoch) Powellism 138
An Eye to the Future 148

BIBLIOGRAPHY 151

INDEX 163

PREFACE

Whilst studying for a master's degree in Modern British Politics at the University of Hull, I came across Friedrich Von Hayek and *The Road to Serfdom* which he published in 1944.

I had commenced my undergraduate studies at Staffordshire University towards the end of Margaret Thatcher's second term in office. At the time, even though I was full of youthful exuberance, I was struck by the effect that Margaret Thatcher had had, and was having on Britain and on the British psyche and how it changed and affected the political, social and economic climate of Britain. As a student I was aware and concerned about the economic and social conditions emerging, which over a relatively short period of time, seemed to engrain inequality, injustice, poverty, unemployment and discontent, within and between regions, communities, families, individuals and the state.

A new dawn of free market economic policies were implemented, and it caused societal pain as demonstrated in the breakdown of law and order between workers and the police during the miners strikes. The flip side of the new economic dawn was the prospect of increased GDP, low inflation, and a more prosperous country. At the time I had an awareness of the importance of Hayek to Margaret Thatcher's programme, and I proceeded to write a paper on the influences of Hayek on Margaret Thatcher.

Over the last three to four years, I have watched with interest the changes and machinations of the Conservative Party, and thirty-one years after penning my paper on Thatcherism and Hayek, I have decided to revisit this in order to provide a wider, a more informed and expansive historical view of the economics of the modern conservative party, its direction(s) of travel, and to explore Margaret Thatcher's application of monetarism and Hayekian free market economics.

The effects of Margaret Thatcher and Thatcherism on society were profound and it still occupies a central place not only in the heart of the conservative party, but in the United Kingdom as a whole.

The views and observations presented in this book reflect much of the prevalent thinking at the time, many of which have been usurped, rendered outdated or surprisingly; some have stood the test of time.

I am hopeful that with the passage of time, distance from some of these events, and my increased knowledge, I will be able to offer this contribution to the body of work on Thatcherism and Hayek and their collective effect and impact on Britain's conservative party in the 20th and 21st centuries.

I have attempted to write a simple, short, and brilliant book. I have been successful in that this book is indeed simple and short: I cannot however, lay claim to brilliance. I hope that the message, deep within this book contributes to making all of our lives better.

INTRODUCTION

Hayek was writing in the immediate aftermath of the devastation of the great wars of the 20th century and the Great Depression. At this time, political thinkers, economists, and philosophers were preoccupied with ensuring that the tribulations that had befell and afflicted western Europe would never again return. As a result, unsurprisingly, proponents of each new economic and political doctrine believed in the rightness of their solutions above all others. Views became entrenched and polarised: east versus west, faith versus secularism, and socialism versus capitalism and free market economics.

Thatcherism, as a political ideology, was the apotheosis of a new paradigm in British politics and economics. The growth of credit, the steady diminution in the utility of cash money, the numerous attempts to restructure the British economy, by rolling back public spending, negatively affected the UK's economy by driving up inflation and unemployment, and reducing growth.

From the moment Mrs Thatcher became the leader of the Conservative Party, she made it clear that she wanted to create the conditions required for the revival that Britain so desperately needed.

The programme of political, economic, and social reform that began under Margaret Thatcher was much more than a simple plan to sell off council houses, privatise government-owned utilities, fight trades unions, and reduce inflation. What she ushered in was a redefinition of the *experiential* role of the state in relation to the citizen and the social contract. The theoretical and ideological underpinning for Thatcherism came from the free market economics of Friedrich Von Hayek, which was in tune with the innate instincts of Mrs Thatcher. The vehicle that she deployed in order to bring about her brand of the free market was monetarism.

While Mrs Thatcher was variously accused of being a populist, or as Professor Stuart Hall famously described her, she was an authoritarian populist; her populism focused on the economics of monetarism and the ideological commitment to the free market.

Today's Conservative Party appears to have moved away from focusing on economics and the free market and has turned its face towards the dogma of populism, which divides, not on economic terms – as there appears to be unanimity of thought in that area - but on core political and social issues. Mrs Thatcher was seeking a new economic paradigm predicated on growth, freedom, and deregulation, which would, and did, bring about long-lasting social, economic, and political change. Margaret Thatcher believed that growth depended on individual and economic spontaneity, and an overbearing and strong state was inimical to that. She appeared to find comfort and solace in the view that a market freed from constraints would provide each citizen with the right to choose their own course of action within a free society.

One of the main, enduring and unrealised lasting impact of Friedrich Von Hayek was that he did more to sear on the minds of politicians, economists, and electorates, the belief that despite socialism's inherent predisposition towards equality and fairness for all; socialism was a danger to western society, because as with the rise of fascism and Nazism in Europe, socialism would bring about the same thing in Britain. In order to head this off, Hayek advocated for a free market and the pre-eminence of a pricing system as opposed to a planned economy,

Introduction

which, in his view, would lead to coercion; limit free choice, stymie economic growth, and ultimately lead to fascism.

Thatcherism attempted to mix the economic liberalism and political ideology of Hayek, with Milton Friedman's monetarism, and merge them with conservative authoritarianism. In doing this, she created a hybrid economic and political ideology called Thatcherism.

'Thatcherism, Hayek & the Political Economics of the Conservative Party', explores this journey in the context of Hayek, the emergence and fear of fascism, Winston Churchill, Enoch Powell, and the modern-day conservative party.

If Thatcherism is the benchmark by which past, current and future Conservative Party leaders measure themselves, it is important for us to explore and understand the economic influences of Thatcherism, what it did in its time, and what it gave birth to for the future.

My hope is that this book will assist in our understanding of the conservative party, and how Margaret Thatcher, followed by the years of austerity under David Cameron, BREXIT under Theresa May and Boris Johnson and the short, but catastrophic premiership of Liz Truss; propelled, what was once the right wing of the modern Conservative Party to its centre ground.

Its longevity in power, has ossified its economic agenda into a strident right-wing populist programme and the modern conservative party appears to have ditched the economy in favour of engaging in cultural wars, promoting nationalism, anti-immigration, anti-welfare provision and silently condoning racism.

The party appears to have splintered into innumerable factions and it no longer brandishes its One Nation credentials which saw it seeking to govern for the betterment of the whole nation. The economy has historically been described as the conservative party's strong suit, but it appears to have ceded that ground and lost its reputation for growth, sound money, and economic competence.

This book looks back at Thatcherism as an economic ideology that successfully countered the prevailing economics of Keynesianism by anchoring itself in the free market economics of Hayek; the monetarism of Milton Friedman and positioned itself as a bulwark against state coercion and fascism.

Society is constantly changing, and as each decade passes, it becomes increasingly difficult to understand how we got here. What we see today, is often obscured by the immediacy and frenetic happenings of the *Right Now*: but we need to look in the rear mirror to understand the context and that there is indeed, nothing new under the sun.

CHAPTER 1

Hayek and his Approach

> "History is either a moral argument with lessons for the here-and-now, or it is merely an accumulation of pointless facts."
> (Marr: 2007, xxviii)

Born in Vienna in 1899, the economist and political philosopher Friedrich Von Hayek made huge contributions to economics, theoretical psychology, and political philosophy. In theoretical psychology, he published *The Sensory Order* in 1952, where he discussed the theory of mind and argued that the mind operated on the contents of consciousness but that those contents themselves could not be consciously known. Hayek also wrote extensive papers and essays on history, such as *The Errors of Constructivism* (1978) and 'Competition as a Discovery Procedure'. His, *The Constitution of Liberty*, was arguably, one of the greatest works on classical liberalism, and has been described as the successor to John Stuart Mill's essay, *On Liberty* (1859). My interest in Hayek stems from his seminal work, *The Road to Serfdom,* which he published in 1944.

Hayek earned doctorates in law in 1921 and political science and economics from the University of Vienna in 1923. In 1927, he became the director of the Austrian Institute for Trade Cycle Research, which he had founded with his mentor and professor at Vienna University, Ludwig Von Mises. At the time, Hayek was, and still is, the best-known advocate of the Austrian School of Economics, which was founded in Vienna in 1871 from the works of Carl Menger, Eugen von Böhm-Bawerk and Friedrich von Wieser.

Hayek's work in the 1920s and 1930s was based on the Austrian theory of business cycles, capital theory, and monetary theory. Like Adam Smith, he argued that the pricing system, i.e., free markets, effectively coordinated people's actions in an unplanned and spontaneous way. The market was not perfect, but it was not intentionally designed, so it evolved slowly as the result of human actions. He understood that imperfections in the market would, from time-to-time result in large numbers of people being unemployed. For Hayek, the cause of this was the actions of central banks increasing the money supply, which, in *Prices and Production* (1931), he argued would drive down interest rates, making credit artificially cheap. This artificially cheap credit would encourage businessmen to make investments that they would otherwise not have made if the price signals were not artificially distorted.

This artificially low interest rate increased the number of investments and investors and led to what the Austrian School of Economics called "malinvestment"— where investment allocation was motivated by an increase in the money supply and the artificially low cost of capital.

In England, Hayek lectured at the London School of Economics and Political Science (LSE) from 1931 to 1950 and was Professor of Economic Science and Statistics. In 1938, he became a British citizen. In 1950, Hayek took up a professorship at the University of Chicago, and from 1962 to 1968, he was professor of economics at the University of Freiburg.

Hayek and Gunnar Myrdal were awarded the Nobel Prize in Economics 'For Works In Economic Theory And Inter-Disciplinary Research' in 1974. The Royal Swedish Academy of Sciences stated that the prize was "for their pioneering work in the theory of money and economic fluctuations and for their penetrating analysis of the interdependence of economic, social and institutional phenomena (Nobel: 1974)."

In the 1930s and 1940s, Hayek's main economic opponent was John Maynard Keynes. In his *General Theory of Employment, Interest, and Money* (1936), Keynes set out the case that full employment was not a natural or inevitable outcome of competitive markets. Keynes challenged classical economic thinking, arguing that '...the postulates of classical theory [were] applicable to special cases only and not to the general case... [Additionally, he argued that] ...the characteristics of the special case assumed by the classical theory happen not to be those of the economic society in which [they] actually live, with the result that teaching is misleading and disastrous if we attempt to apply it to the facts of experience' (Keynes: 2009, 5). Classical economic theory believed that full employment was evidence of an undistorted labour market and a reflection of economic equilibrium. However, Keynes believed that market distortions were an undesirable part of competitive markets, as these distortions led to booms and busts. The remedy for Keynes was that governments needed to adopt policies aimed at countering those distortions to ensure full employment because the level of employment was determined by the level of aggregate demand, not by the price of labour, as was believed by the classical economists Jean-Baptiste Say. *Say's Law*, postulated that the production/supply of goods created its own demand, leading to full employment without the need for government intervention because in a market economy with unemployment, workers would be willing to work below the prevailing wage levels.

Hayek and his fellow Austrian students believed that the Keynesian approach and solution were inflationary because, in order to keep unemployment low, the central bank would have to increase the money supply, which would then cause inflation.

Based on the experience of Britain, Western Europe and the United States; it is now widely accepted that Hayek's analysis was correct. It is important to note, however, that this does not necessarily mean that Keynes's diagnosis and solution were wholly incorrect. As in all things in economics, this is as much about sentiment, emotions and also empirically, about the actual volume, or percentage increase in the extra supply of money and whether it leads to inflation, rather than the aggressive assumption that all, and any increase in money supply will inexorably, lead to inflation rising. Secondly, if increasing the money supply did lead to a temporary hike in inflation, how long would that last, and crucially, what were/are the economic stabilisers that a government has to counter this?

Hayek argued that both inflation and deflation produced peculiar effects. By causing unexpected price changes, both were bound to disappoint, firstly because prices prove to be higher or lower than they were expected, and secondly, as more sooner happens, these price changes come to be expected and cease to have the effect that their unforeseen occurrence had. The difference between inflation and deflation is that with inflation, the pleasant surprise comes first and the negative later: while with deflation, the first effect on business is distressing.

The War, the Nazis and the Fall of European Communism

The years during and after the Great Depression (1929 – 1941) was a period of great economic and political introspection. At the height of the depression in 1935, John Maynard Keynes published The *General Theory of Employment, Interest, and Money*, in which he argued against the notion that governments should be laissez-faire and that the market would correct itself on its own, creating or leading to full employment. For Keynes, government intervention in the nation's economy was essential during periods of slow or negative economic growth, and governments should resist the temptation to underinvest but should invest in order to stimulate growth and stave off lower levels of consumption than expected or anticipated. Keynes's theory was widely accepted as there was seemingly no viable alternative given the parlour state of the UK's and the USA's economy after the first war. Hayek, drawing from the work of his mentor Ludwig von Mises, who was at the University of Vienna, argued a counter position to Keynes, which was that market freedoms and the free exchange of goods and services were essential for a successful economy based on real knowable costs. Hayek drew on Mises, who had argued in the 1920s that one needed to know the real price and costs of things as this was the only way to decide on the allocation of resources. Hayek, taking this a step further, said that the real price and costs of things could only be known by allowing the market to be free. Specifically, Hayek maintained that this could only be achieved by utilising the free exchange of goods and services and then allowing this discovery process to inform the price system. In the early 1920s, this position, postulated by Mises and then built on by Hayek, was gaining momentum until the Great Depression, when western countries found that they needed to proactively jump start their economies, having just come out of the First World War which had started in 1914 and ended in 1918.

Hayek observed that socialists in Britain were advocating some of the same welfare policies that he had seen implemented in Germany in the 1920s. This, for Hayek, was a dangerous move that would ultimately result in totalitarianism and coercive government control over people's lives. In response, he wrote *The Road to Serfdom* in 1944 as a warning against this and launched an excoriating attack on collectivism, and *The Road to Serfdom* was offered as an explanation for the rise of Nazism in Germany. Hayek argued that the German people were people of goodwill and that prior to the rise of Adolf Hitler, they were tolerant and people of good will and intentions. It was however the pursuit of socialism and socialist policies that prepared the way for Nazism. He argued that collectivism, whether in the USA, Germany, the Soviet Union, or Britain, would erode, cut away, and undermine personal liberty and freedom, ultimately resulting in authoritarianism. Hayek was clear that it was not self-interest or evil intentions that motivated many intellectuals towards socialism; they were motivated by honest convictions. The intellectuals that Hayek referred to were not academic intellectuals, and they definitely were not experts, but they were people who had time to think, read, and write. Collectivism or socialism didn't grow up from working-class people, it came from intellectuals, people whom Hayek called "second-hand dealers in ideas". By 1949, when he wrote *The Intellectuals and Socialism,* Hayek concluded that the 'Second-hand Dealers in Ideas', we're dominant.

At the heart of his argument on liberty, which we will discuss later, was his wish to prevent coercion. For example, he saw planning as leading to dictatorship, as dictatorship was the most effective instrument for coercion (Hayek, 2001:91). In order for the government to give one person money, it must take it from another, and it must take it forcibly first through the system of taxation. The promise of socialists was that there was a new form of attainable freedom. In the past, freedom was related to freedom from coercion and freedom from the arbitrary power of office. However, "[the] new freedom [that the socialists were aiming for] was merely another name for power or wealth" and what the promise really amounted to was "…that the existing disparities in the range of choice of different people were to disappear. The demand for new freedom was the demand for an equal distribution of wealth. The promise of greater freedom has become one of the greatest weapons of social propaganda and it seemed that what was promised to us as the road to freedom was in fact the high road to servitude" (Hayek, 2001:26-2). But even while doing this, collectivists, socialists, and those in favour of planned economies cannot ignore the fact that free markets produce wealth: they therefore attack free markets on grounds of morals, greed and selfishness. However, for Hayek, free markets, should be welcomed, for without them, there cannot be personal liberty, property rights, or the rule of law (Hayek: 1982).

The provision of the welfare state during times of hardship and the Great Depression was central to the way the US and Great Britain supported their citizens through this difficult time. However, national socialism was a doctrine used in Nazi Germany and by the fascists in Italy (Hayek, 2010: 171). What Hayek did was align the two approaches and say that the United States and Great Britain had adopted a similar approach to economic and social problems as Nazi Germany and Fascist Italy. Hayek had equated the welfare state responses of Great Britain and the United States of America with the national socialism of Nazi Germany and Fascist Italy. In reality, Hayek was applying a theoretical Weberian ideal type to a real-life experience. In the wake of what Hitler had done, this annoyed western economists and politicians, and served to discredit the work of Friedrich von Hayek. At the heart of Hayek's view was that distrusting the market and having no interest in individual decision-making necessitated that the state, as a strongman, would control individuals and the market. This, he argued, was similar to fascism and the Nazi approach, which had been so clearly defeated. It is clear that Hayek chose to make this stark contrast because he wanted to demonstrate the pathological and undesirable nature and conclusion of state-controlled planned economies. His conflation of socialism with fascism and Nazism was deemed unacceptable, and his approach of starkly polarising the economic debate, associating the political left – however unintentional- with having a scintilla of common purpose with a dark period in European history pushed his work and him into the shadows, and for decades, Hayek and his work was rarely read or spoken of. It was primarily for this reason that Keynes and Keynesianism became preeminent in the 20th century. It is, however, worth noting that the association of socialism with coercive authoritarianism, illiberalism and anti-Semitism has never entirely gone away, and the political right has – to this day - often seized on this, pointing accusatory fingers and gas-lighting the electorate to varying degrees that the political and economic plans of the left should be feared.

Hayek has been widely cited and credited for his impact on Margaret Thatcher and his wider impact and contribution to western political economics; however, he should also be held responsible for doing more than any other economist, politician, or political thinker, to crystalise in the minds of electorates in Great Britain and the USA the belief and the opinion that socialism – despite its inherent leanings towards equality and fairness for all – is a danger to western society. At the age of ninety-nine, in his book *The Fatal Conceit: The Errors of Socialism* (1988) he outlined that the intellectuals' attraction to socialism was deeply flawed because the 'strong belief prevails that the influence of the intellectuals on politics is negligible. Yet over somewhat longer periods, they have probably never exercised such great influence (Hayek: 1949, 371). The intellectuals he described were predisposed to socialism primarily because they were theorists rather than doers. Hayek references Schumpeter, who in *Capitalism, Socialism, and Democracy* (1942) stated that it is the absence of direct responsibility for practical affairs and the absence of first-hand knowledge that distinguishes intellectuals from other people. While it may be empirically unsound, anecdotally; those on the political left seem to have a greater propensity to have intellectuals and academics with a greater awareness of injustice and a wish to challenge the way things are than those who are typically on the right of politics. Hayek believes that there is no ill intent and that the intellect is driven by good intentions and has no self-interest tendencies. The problem is that they make an error as they judge information and evidence, not on its own merits but on whether it fits into the general principles and concepts that they hold (Hayek: 1949, 376). This is where we see the stark dividing lines of Hayek's concept of the political left and right. This became, and has remained a foundational position of the right, and Thatcherism.

The Collapse of Eastern European Governments

Communism Collapses in Eastern Europe

This fear was not entirely irrational, or void of real-world evidence. The emergence, growth, and catastrophic collapse of communist Eastern European governments in the 1990s can be traced back to events immediately preceding and during the 1917 Russian Revolution.

In the decades leading up to 1917, Russia was experiencing difficulties economically, militarily, socially, and politically. 19 centuries, Russia was a rural agricultural country, populated by peasants and former landowners using traditional methods of farming.

Due to poverty, the dawn of the 20th century saw large swathes of Russia's rural labour force move to urban areas as Russia began to industrialise. This mass movement of rural people to towns, created problems of overcrowding, poor and unsafe working conditions, low wages, and at this time, workers had little, if any, rights. This situation was made worse because Russia sought to increase its territorial influence over Korea and Manchuria and refused to withdraw from Manchuria as agreed in September 1901 in the Xinchou Treaty (Boxer Protocol or Peace Agreement between the Great Powers and China). To the surprise of the Tsar, Japan launched a surprise attack in 1904, winning numerous major battles against the great European state (Jukes: 1914). The costs to Russia were huge financially, emotionally, and seriously affected the international status of the once great country. As the economy faltered and poverty increased, the discontent of workers resulted in riots and strikes for better conditions and pay. Public disorder increased, and the stability of the old order came increasingly under attack.

The turning point for Russia was in 1905 when soldiers of the Imperial Guard shot unarmed demonstrators as they marched towards the Winter Palace in St. Petersburg to present a petition to Tsar Nicholas II. This event became known as Red (Bloody) Sunday. Previous to this, the Tsar had been resistant to social reform of any sort, but Red (Bloody) Sunday forced Nicholas to create the October Manifesto, which decreed limited civil rights, and establish the democratically elected parliament called the Duma.

The First World War did not change the war fortunes of Russia; and as in Manchuria, the Tsar's military prowess was found wanting. The Tsar demonstrated poor decision-making and failed to provide adequate provision for troops. The Tsar's authority was further seriously undermined in 1915 when, as commander in chief of the army, he went to the Eastern Front to lead the Imperial Russian Army. As the commander in chief, leading his troops, he in battle, he was held personally responsible for the significant failures of his military. In addition to this; when he left for the Eastern Front, he left his wife, Tsarina Alexandra (who was also Princess Alexandra of Hesse-Darmstadt, - a Dutchy in Germany) in charge. Due to her German heritage (because the Germans were the foes of the Russians), Tsarina was treated with suspicion and was unpopular. Adding to the distrust and suspicion. Tsarina had a strong friendship, dependency, and, and possibly, intimate relationship with the Siberian monk Grigori Rasputin, whose personal reputation as a monk, faith healer, and mystic was met with much concern and scepticism. Rasputin exercised considerable control over her on important government decisions, which the Russians disliked. This resulted in his assassination by Russian aristocrats in 1916. Coupled with Tsar Nicholas's absence, his government was undermined and weakened. During the First World War almost 2 million Russian soldiers were killed. Russia suffered multiple defeats, and many of the Tzars officers were killed and replaced by conscripts who had no loyalty to him. The increasing loss of lives and military defeats led to revolts and mutinies.

The wartime demand on the Russian population was as extensive as it had been in Manchuria. Russia's factories needed to produce war supplies, and large sections of the male population were conscripted into the army, which meant that there were labour shortages in the factories and many strikes due to poor pay and conditions. The migration of rural workers and peasants to the cities made the situation worse as the new arrivals were not equipped for city life, and the rural areas from where they had left, consequently had a shortage of workers, negatively affecting the production of food. A counter movement of workers from the city to the rural areas in search of food began because the demands of the war necessitated that produce be sent to the military first, and so the railways were unavailable to transport food stuff to the cities.

By 1915, the strain on the Russian economy was so great that the government began to print money, which led to high inflation. Tsar Nicholas was at the Eastern Front and unable to quell the strikes, the general dissent, and the unrest. Revolutionary groups gained strength and prominence as they argued that the Tsar's rule should come to an end and the people or workers should take over. In commemoration of the events of Bloody Sunday in 1905, there were more riots, disturbances, and strikers; and in February 1917, strikers from the Putilov engineering plant joined the celebration of International Women's Day when some of the forces of Tsar Nicholas II again opened fire on the protestors (Irvine: 2020). The Cossack soldiers refused to fire and joined the protesters against the Tsar. Meanwhile, the Tsar attempted to return to St. Petersburg; he was prevented from doing so and was forced to abdicate, and a provisional government was put in place. Even with the abdication of Tsar Nicholas, all was not well. The Bolsheviks – who were later renamed the Communist Party, led by Vladimir Lenin, did not respect the legitimacy of the provisional government and in October 1917 they arrested members of the government, seized power and in 1918, the Tsar and his family were executed.

Part of the legacy of this time was that since the 1917 Russian Revolution, communism has dominated not only Russia but all the states that formed the Soviet Union. Vladimir Lenin was the first leader of the Soviet Union, officially the Union of Soviet Socialist Republics (USSR) which was a federal system of fifteen republics: Armenia, Azerbaijan, Belarus, Kazakhstan, Lithuania, Estonia, Georgia, Russia, Kyrgyzstan, Latvia, Moldova, Tajikistan, Ukraine, Uzbekistan, and Turkmenistan. With a population of 290,000,000 people, the Soviet Union lasted from 1922 to 1991. National Socialism was the political ideology that Lenin believed would ultimately lead to communism. After Lenin's death in

1924, Joseph Stalin took power and grew the Soviet economy rapidly by rolling out a programme of industrialisation. His strategy and his push to collectivism also led to famine, which saw millions die between 1930 and 1933. Communism dominated not only Russia but the Soviet bloc until December 1991.

The Soviet Union had the world's largest arsenal of nuclear weapons; the largest standing military; was a founding member of the United Nations; was one of the five permanent members of the United Nations Security Council; and was the world's second-largest economy. Even with these impressive statistics, there was a problem at the heart of the Soviet Union. Russia had huge supplies of oil and gas, and when oil prices shot up in the 1970s, Russia was able to export and build its reserves. The problem that Russia had was that it was too dependent on its natural resources, and in the 1980s, the economy began to stagnate due to its outdated manufacturing and mining techniques. World oil prices fluctuated markedly, and in 1986, they collapsed, causing the income and standard of living of the Soviet people to fall considerably in comparison to people in the West. The Cold War with the West saw the USSR spend huge amounts on military hardware, and it began to print money, which increased inflation and poverty. Political and economic change was needed, and after becoming General Secretary of the Communist Party of the Soviet Union in 1985, Mikhail Gorbachev became leader and committed to stemming the economic decline. Gorbachev heralded in a new era of Perestroika and Glasnost. Perestroika was about removing centralised control and allowing a freer market to develop. Glasnost, on the other hand, centred around freedom of speech: the press were allowed greater freedom, and dissidents were released from prison. Corruption, which was a well-known aspect of life, was exposed, and USSR citizens began to experience a level of freedom and autonomy that they, until then, did not think was possible.

Unlike Leonid Brezhnev, Gorbachev didn't see the need for the USSR to impose itself militarily, and therefore he resisted the temptation to intervene in countries where socialist rule was under threat. The result was that democratic elections in Eastern European countries led to non-communist leaders like Lech Walesca being elected in June 1989 as Poland's first non-communist president. Other developments included the border between Hungary and Austria being removed; a number of Baltic states were slowly and inexorably moving towards independence; and possibly the most significant development was the fall of the Berlin Wall in November 1989: the Iron Curtain had finally come down.

The collapse of east European communist governments in 1989, the dissolution of the Soviet Union, and the creation of Russia made academics, economists, and politicians realise that the promises of communism to bring fairness and fair distribution of wealth via a planned economy were unrealistic. The irony was that there was very little in-principal rejection that, if properly implemented, socialism had the potential to offer up a more equal and fair distribution of wealth. What was however clear from the collapse of European communist governments was that the version of socialism offered was undeliverable, ineffective and was unable to deliver the fairness and fair distribution that were supposedly the hallmarks of a system that was markedly different from the hitherto exploitative and unfair free market systems in operation mainly in the West. Hayek, however, argued that disorder was the only logical and indeed inevitable outcome of socialism, where governments planned their economies in the absence of pricing which reflected supply and demand, e.g., the preferences of people.

The collapse of Eastern European communist governments presaged the beginning of the end of one economic experiment and the dominance and rise of new thinking in economics, government, and politics.

Hayek. An ideological Leap to the Future

Knowledge, Competitive Markets and Price Signals

Hayek's influence on western economics and Thatcherism cannot be properly understood without looking at his seminal work which formed the bedrock of his concepts of liberty, coercion, and free markets. Hayek's foundational thesis, *The Use of Knowledge in Society* (1945) set out how information and knowledge informed decision-making. This is where we find the foundations for his further thinking and writing.

The title of Hayek's 1974 Nobel Memorial lecture was *The Pretence of Knowledge*. In this speech, Professor Hayek explained that there was an inability in the ability of economists to guide policy more successfully because they tended to erroneously imitate the procedures of the physical sciences – an attempt which if applied to social sciences, and economics in particular, is likely to lead to outright error (Horn: 2009, 308). Hayek added that the economic theories of Keynes had been accepted by columnists and especially politicians because of the supposed link between total demand and total employment, which was confirmed -or seemed to be so - by statistical evidence. This was therefore accepted as the only important cause or connection. In contrast, the theory held by Hayek in the 1930s was, for him, the correct and only real explanation for unemployment. Alas, as it could not be supported by statistical evidence; this for Hayek, led to the fantasy of scientism and what he called the *pretence of knowledge*.

The error of science for him was that it supposes that the methods of the physical sciences, where causes are normally measurable, can be shifted to the social sciences, where there are essentially complex phenomena arising from very large numbers that are rarely observable or directly measurable. As far as Hayek was concerned, economists had been led into the fiction that only measurable factors were relevant to policy. In *Full Employment at Any Price* (1975:30) Professor Hayek was strongly critical of the general misuse of macro-methods and mathematics, which refused to recognise that while we can explain general patterns of development, we cannot in the social sciences determine or predict the numerical values of individual events. Politicians, policymakers, and economists were, erroneously for Hayek, applying scientific methods mechanically and uncritically to fields different from those in which those scientific processes had been formed.

In *The Use of Knowledge in Society* (1945), Hayek presented his central concern about knowledge; which was that no person, individual, or series of entities could possess' complete knowledge of the present; let alone the future. Hayek was concerned that governments in the west were increasingly deciding to centrally manage and plan their economies: this, for him, was not the answer or an antidote to the vacuum of knowledge. For Hayek, the most efficient system was one that accepted that no single entity or series of groupings could know what was happening in the economy – with any degree of certainty or accuracy. He therefore asserted that a network of competitive markets would provide the answer, as competition would send price signals and information relevant to the present situation. This, in-turn, would force individuals and entities to respond in predictable ways to ensure their success in the competitive market. Hayek argued in *The Road to Serfdom* (1944) that the price system will fulfil its function if competition prevails and if producers have to adapt to price changes. This, for Hayek, was preferable to a centrally controlled, planned economy. In 1962, Milton Friedman, in *Capitalism and Freedom*, echoed Hayek's views when he outlined that the basic problem of organisations was how to coordinate the economic activities of large numbers of people (Friedman, 1962. 12). For Friedman, only a free market could coordinate this knowledge, or amount of information.

Hayek was not saying that the market was flawless and that it would always provide maximum results for participants, in the same way that one cannot predict how people will respond to incentives created within a centrally planned economy. In *Law, Legislation, and Liberty* (1973), Hayek quotes Adam Smith, who observed that there were technocrats who did not appreciate that they could not direct individuals in a predictably deterministic way (Hayek: 1973).

For Adam Smith, these technocrats were the "man of system" who believed that they could arrange and manage society as easily as one moved chess pieces on a chess board. The distinction and difference with a chess piece is that they have no other purpose save to be moved by the hand and to remain until moved again. However, individuals in society have self-determination and can move at will, whether rationally or irrationally. 'Although different from that which the legislature might choose to impress upon it, if those two principles coincide and act in the same direction, the game of human society will go on easily and harmoniously and is very likely to be happy and successful. If they are opposite or different, the game will go on miserably, and society [will] be at the highest degree of disorder' (Smith: 1790, 234).

The system has a logic that planners cannot change; as such, the decision was whether to work with that logic or against it; which for Smith was a choice between harmony and misery. Planners who disregarded economic logic were consciously deciding to sacrifice their 'pawns': this was something a person of true benevolence would not do (Smith: 1790).

Hayek's objection to central planning was not only the Smithian challenge that information is too widely dispersed and therefore hard to acquire; but additionally, that sufficient information and knowledge were impossible for any individual or committee to acquire because the knowledge was not only dispersed, but also incomplete and contradictory (Hayek. 1945, 519). If a central planner with limited and arbitrary information sets prices rather than the prices being set spontaneously by consumers and producers, who are typically the only people to have that information in reliable and timely form, those artificially set prices will be less reliable and less timely and have the potential to distort the market. Hayek is at pains to point out that few possess all the relevant information; if we can start out with a given system of preferences and if we command complete knowledge of available means, the problem that remains is purely one of logic (Hayek 1945, 519).

Soviet central planners made decisions by checking prices on international markets. What Hayek was intimating here is that we are never and can never be at the place where the sum of all the parts relies on the application of pure logic. The reason for this is that the "data" from which the economic calculus starts, is never given to a single mind who could work out the implications for the whole of society (Hayek: 1945, 519).

The challenge for those who would seek to plan economies is brought to life in the instance where there is no market information but there is demand for a particular product. The question for the planner is how should they decide whether to direct producers to make more of one product and less of others and what proportion of raw materials should be reserved for other uses (Schmidtz and Boettke: 2021, 3).

The conundrum for planners, as Hayek saw it, was that when consumers are not paying for what they receive, their demand is effectively infinite. In these instances, it was inevitable that a central planner's task would become one of cost containment. Worse yet; a planner with no measure of cost has only a limited basis for deciding what to count as containing cost. If a given tonne of steel can make one car or ten refrigerators, which way of using steel is more economical? How does a planner decide whether to invest in upgrading water supplies or nuclear reactors? If all you know as a producer is that people are asking for infinitely more than you can give; eventually you turn a deaf ear, deliver your quota, and pay no attention to whether demands from below (from customers) are being met. The only demands that have consequences are those from above (which is, those which come to you through your supervisors) (Schmidtz and Boettke: 2021, 3). Hayek states that "only prices determined on the free market will bring [about the situation] that demand equals supply" (Hayek: 1960,63). Price controls – floors and ceilings -make buyers and sellers less able to respond to the signals they would send each other if they could raise their offer or lower their asking price. If prices cannot rise, then buyers cannot signal to producers that demand has increased and that producers would sell more if they were to increase supply; if producers do not increase supply, rising demand results in shortages rather than economic growth (Schmidtz and Boettke: 2021). Hayek's baseline position in relation to this was that if a product is readily available on the market, it is because it has been overpriced by the central planner, leading to consumers no longer buying it. The oversupply results in the planner buying up the product, subsidising it, and selling or giving it to the citizen free or at a heavily discounted price. Citizens end up paying the higher price anyway, indirectly through taxes. As consumers, citizens are thwarted, and as taxpayers, they are impoverished (Hayek: 1945,527).

When Hayek published *'Use of Knowledge'* in 1945, Gordon E. Moore's law was not only unknown, (Moore came up with this principle on transistors as Co- founder of Intel in 1965) but computational technology had not really gotten underway in any large-scale systematic way; and where it was in operational use, it was not a ubiquitous resource capable of informing, anticipating or analysing market signals and therefore its use didn't preoccupy economists, investors, politicians, social and political scientists in the way that it does now. Even today, computers are unable to solve the problem that Hayek was articulating because the solving of the problem is not primarily due to a lack of processing power but a lack of knowing and knowledge (Schmidtz and Boettke: 2021. How can any entity or grouping know enough? Access to the huge swathe of information contained in the millions of interactions between individuals as they trade on facts, sentiment, hope, and fear, was, and is impossible. With the growth and ubiquity of technology, this problem – which is now restricted or stymied by limitations in computing and processing power – still exists. At its core, no one knows how to control societal outcomes because outcomes are determined more by unintended consequences than by the realisation of designed political outcomes.

It is important to state that while Hayek pushes against central planning and any leanings towards a *'strong man'*: he is not asserting that free and competitive markets are perfect, stable, or that they will lead inexorably to prosperity. Hayek was aware that the self-interested nature of competition meant that knowledge was constantly changing as buyers and sellers responded to market signals, creating equilibrium and disequilibrium, with agents ultimately acting in their own self-interest. This is what creates innovation based on knowable knowledge: it also carries within it the 'freedom to fail' which is an essential aspect of this rational economic order; for no single agent can know everything.

Keynes, too, was interested in the economic effects of knowledge on investments. In the early 20th century, after the 1st World War and in the period during and immediately after the Great Depression, the stage was set for academic pugilism, which saw Friedrich Von Hayek and John Maynard Keynes squaring off. In *"The State of Long-Term Expectation"* in *The General Theory of Employment, Interest, and Money* (1935), John Maynard Keynes argued - correctly - that future events were unknown and unknowable: yet investors made present-day decisions armed with optimism and *inductive projection,* where they drew conclusions about future events using specific observations, applying general principles and probability to inform their decisions, or using optimism or scepticism for particular courses of action or inaction. However, optimism could be dashed in a moment and investment decisions altered to the detriment of society; resulting in crashes, mass unemployment, and other forms of market failure. One of the central tenets of Keynesian economics was that governments cannot and should not rely on monetary policy to counter the effects of market/investor sentiment because sentiment could often leave the market and, by extension – the economy unstable and highly unpredictable. Keynes maintained that at times of uncertainty, governments ought to step in to play a central role in the economy by filling the gaps, restoring public confidence, and maintaining confidence in the nation's economy. Keynes was also concerned about future knowledge – and lack of knowledge - and the economic effects of that knowledge because we pass from the knowledge of proposition *a*, to the knowledge of proposition *b* through a logical relationship between them (Keynes, 1921: 12-13).

Hayek and Keynes both saw flaws in human knowledge and how ignorance of prices and unknowable markets affected decision-making. Ignorance is at the heart of what we can do because we cannot know everything. However, Keynes and Hayek came to different conclusions. For Hayek, government intervention in free markets through subsidies and taxation created distortions and disequilibrium.

Hayek cites, as an example, times when governments reduced interest rates. While he uses the term 'artificially' reduced; the definition of 'artificially reduced requires some definition. For example, as a result of the global financial crisis of 2008, interest rates in the United Kingdom had been at a historic low of 0.5 percent in March 2009 and 0.25 percent in August 2016. The interest rate rose slightly back to 0.5 percent by November 2017 and then increased to 0.75 percent in August 2018 (UK Finance: 2023).

In August 2023, the Bank of England's Monetary Policy Committee (MPC) increased the Bank's base interest rate by 0.25 percentage points up to 5.25 percent, and as predicted by Hayek, investors who had exposed themselves to the market in the previous 10 years became overstretched as interest rates soared, making their once affordable enterprises unsustainable, resulting in mass bankruptcies and unemployment. Those who had purchased property or were remortgaging their homes began to find that the effects of the increased interests rates made their repayments unaffordable, resulting in an increase in home repossessions. In quarter 3 of 2023, there were 87,930 homeowner mortgages in arrears of 2.5 percent or more of the outstanding balance. This was 7 percent greater than in the previous quarter. Within the total of 87,930, there were 34,110 homeowner mortgages in the lightest arrears band (representing between 2.5 and 5 percent of the outstanding balance). This was 10 percent greater than in the previous quarter (UK Finance: 2023). This essentially meant that 53,820 homeowners were in more serious arrears above 5 percent of the outstanding balance. Hayek argued that the same thing effects public sector and government infrastructure spending. The government artificially supports spending, but when it withdraws its spending, negative consequences ensue, placing governments in the insidious position of being tempted to maintain spending, thereby distorting the market. For Hayek, governments must resist this temptation.

The challenge for the government, however, is whether they leave their citizens in despair and poverty or whether they take the step of supporting citizens during times of hardship. This was at the heart of the post-war debate that nation-states were having, and having observed what had happened in Germany and Italy, Hayek feared that a similar thing was happening in Britain.

What Hayek had identified, and offered up as a solution was what Max Weber would describe as an ideal type. Hayek's accentuation of the benefits and the potency of a pricing system, the absence of coercion, access to free markets and the exchange of goods and services, would, in Hayek's mind create the conditions for freedom and economic growth which would not be possible in a socialist or collectivist state. Hayek was guarding and warning against a central planning and an overbearing state attempting to implement its will with insufficient knowledge. As Weber explained in *The Protestant Ethic and the Spirit of Capitalism*, ideal types were constructed from elements that exist in reality but they are conceptual in that they cannot be found in the described configuration anywhere in the real world. This is important because attempts to implement Hayekian political economics would unavoidably collide with the reality of the real world and the plurality of competing interests within it. As the former boxer Mike Tyson famously said, everyone has a plan until they get punched in the mouth; or as the former conservative British Prime Minister, Harold Macmillan said, when asked what could push the government's agenda off course, he responded: "Events, dear boy, events".

CHAPTER 2

One Nation, Churchill and the Conservative Party

Political reality, opportunism, or expediency will always feature highly in the decisions that politicians and governments make. In 1845, Benjamin Disraeli's book, *Sybil*, subtitled *The Two Nations*, was an upper-class romance novel and also a political manifesto. The book was, in part, a response to the crisis of industrialisation and the first wave of industrial revolutions in England in the 1840s. In this best seller, Disraeli depicted the plight of the working classes, women and children. He highlighted the low wages, the poor conditions of housing and work and the misery of industrial towns. Written against the background of the Chartist movement, it exposed the darker side of the prosperity of Victorian England, contrasting the luxurious life of the aristocracy with the extreme poverty and social instability of industrial and agricultural workers in and around the expanding industrial towns of England. Disraeli charted the poverty and inequality that had appeared in Britain between the rich and the poor, and he criticised the rapid and uncontrolled wave of industrialisation as the immoral byproduct of laissez-faire economics, which had created what he described as the appearance of two nations. Disraeli saw these two nations as posing an existential threat to the future of the Tory party, and something needed to be done about it.

While Disraeli was the originator of the description and identification of two nations living in Britain, he never used the phrase one nation. It was Prime Minister Stanley Baldwin, in a speech at the Albert Hall in December 1924, who said that the Tory party needed to make one nation of the two nations that Benjamin Disraeli had written about.

Disraeli (and indeed, others) identified that there was a reform agenda possible that could see the conservative party as being a friend of the working class, acknowledging that the working class was proud of belonging to a great country. This resulted in the conservative government - on the urging of the Liberals - introducing the Second Parliamentary Reform Act in 1867, which significantly widened the franchise and almost immediately increased working-class support for the conservatives. The 1884 Reform Act further widened the franchise and was the first electoral reform act to apply to the whole United Kingdom. The Reform Act of 1918 granted voting rights to women, and in 1928, the last piece of gender discrimination was removed by the conservatives under the Equal Franchise Act of 1928.

In addition to drawing inspiration from Disraeli's *'Sybil'*; One Nation conservatism was also exemplified by Harold Macmillan's book on political philosophy, *'The Middle Way'*, (1930), and Lord Hailsham's *'The Conservative Cases'*, (1959), which had themes of people being divided by function but organically unified in the nation. The overriding duty of Disraeli, Macmillan, and Lord Hailsham was to preserve the unity of the nation.

Winston Churchill didn't use the phrase One Nation, but the social reforms that Churchill supported - as we will see - entitle him to be described as a One Nation conservative even though the reforms occurred when he was a member of a liberal government, at a time when the conservatives opposed the agenda. Paradoxically, while the famous conservative leader and Conservative premier was known for his wartime record, he was also variously described and credited as being [a key] architect of the welfare state and became a key proponent of One Nation Conservatism (Marshall and Porion: 2023, 81).

Churchill, too, bought in to the need for a conservative-led programme of social reform. At the turn of the century, free trade was the defining issue in British politics. While writing the biography of his father, - Lord Randolph Churchill, Chancellor of the Exchequer in 1886 - Winston Churchill's belief grew that his father was correct in his belief that Conservatives could only prosper if they were a party of social reform (Marshall and Porion: 2023, 81. Churchill's two-volume biography of his father, Lord Randolph, led him to conclude that the Conservative government was indeed betraying his father's legacy by shifting away from free trade and becoming protectionist and reactionary rather than reforming. Winston Churchill was a social reformer, and the refocus of the conservatives away from free trade to protectionism did not sit well with him. In 1904, Churchill crossed the floor of the House of Commons and joined the liberal party.

This was the beginnings of the concept of One Nationism in the conservative party, which later grew into a cogent movement. After the defeat of the conservatives in the 1950 general election, nine newly-elected backbench MPs, including Edward Heath, Angus Maude, Iain Macleod, Robert Carr, Reginald Maulding, and the founding members, Cuthbert Alport and Angus Maude, and later Enoch Powell, presented new approaches to conservative party policies on the welfare state and poverty in post-war Britain. This one-nation group held on to Disraeli's view that the Tory Party was a national party and that it could not succeed if it presided over or enabled a divided nation.

In order to maintain their independence, it was agreed that members of the one-nation group had to be backbenchers. If any member was appointed as a minister, a whip, or assumed any government position, they would have to leave the group, but they were free to resume their position in the One Nation Group when that person returned to the backbenches or after the conservatives lost power through a general election. The One Nation Group of conservatives focused their attention on the welfare state and social policies in the 1950s and rejected universal benefits, which the labour party and the left saw as necessary. As a sign of things to come, housing was seen as an important sector, and Enoch Powell wrote a chapter on housing in which he called for the ending of rent caps so that landlords could ask for higher rents, and they accepted welfare spending as long as expenditure was managed and controlled. The programme of denationalisation of state-run entities was one way of engraining and crystallising a reduction in public spending. This programme of privatisation and marketisation has ever since been at the core of *New Right* ideology and have become articles of faith, as they marked a strategic departure from the dominance of Keynesian economics.

The Conservative Party has dominated British politics in the 19th, 20th, and most of the 21st centuries, firstly because it quickly identified that its success lay in understanding and accepting that despite their own wealth and privilege, the United Kingdom was not only one nation, but the populace viewed itself as such. Secondly, the conservative party implemented policies that spoke to this agenda, and increased and widened the franchise through the Parliamentary Reform Acts from 1867. The party was, and indeed, saw itself as the natural governing party of the United Kingdom and the evidence appears to bear this out. Since 1923 and 2024, the Conservative Party have provided the United Kingdom with 14 individuals who became prime minister, - 3 of whom (Boris Johnson, Liz Truss and Rishi Sunak) entered office following the resignation of their predecessors. In contrast, over the same 100 years, the Labour Party has provided only 6 individuals who became prime minister, - only 1 entered office following the resignation of their predecessor. Thirdly, until recently, (2015) the conservative party appeared to be a cohesive, a one nation group of conservatives including all wings of the conservative party, from those who advocated for a more limited role for the state, i.e., free market advocates, to those on the more socially liberal wing calling for a more interventionist state. The comfortable juxtaposition of the conservative family under one banner has in recent years become fractured as divisions and culture wars have raged on issues around immigration, faith, gender and Britain's exit from the European Union. These have threatened the hegemony of the conservative party in British politics.

Free Trade

Free trade had been a longstanding contentious issue in the conservative party. In 1846, in the aftermath of the great famine in Ireland, Tory Prime Minister Sir Robert Peel took an unprecedented step and repealed the protectionist Corn Laws, thereby allowing foreign corn to flow freely into the country. The Tory party was fiercely protectionist, and Robert Peel was only able to repeal the Corn Laws with the support of the Whig opposition in his own party.

By way of conservative party history; the Whig faction constantly battled with the Tories for power and merged into the Liberal Party. Later, some Whigs broke away and formed the Liberal Unionist Party, which merged into the Conservative Party in 1912.

In a similar vein, in 2024, there are numerous divisions in the modern conservative party who have been described as coalescing around five families which pivot between factions on the right represented by the European Research Group (ERG) which was instrumental in steering the mood music during Britain's exit of the European Union (BREXIT); the Northern Research Group (NRG) established after the 2019 election victory to ensure that the promises to the Red Wall were delivered under One Nation Conservatism and others.

Sir Robert Peel's decision to repeal the Corn Laws and. By way of history; the Whig faction constantly battled with the Tories for power and merged into the Liberal Party. Later, some Whigs broke away and formed the Liberal Unionist Party, which merged into the Conservative Party in 1912. Sir Robert Peel's decision to allow the free flow of food cost him dearly, and while he was successful in repealing the Corn Laws in June 1846, on the same day, his Irish Coercion Bill was defeated, and he resigned as prime minister, having served in that office twice between 1834 - 1835 and 1841 - 1846. After Peel's resignation, the Tories were out of power for a generation. The disunity around free trade, which saw Winston Churchill defect from the conservative party, caused the Conservative & Unionist Party to lose the 1906 election to a Liberal landslide. In addition to the conservative party's position on free trade, the need for social reform weighed heavily on Churchill.

In his first York study, *Poverty: A Study of Town Life* (1901) Seebohm Rowntree studied the living conditions of poor people in York. His researchers visited every working class household and revealed that the poverty in York was structural and the result of low wages, poor health and living conditions: it was not due to laziness or moral reasons. His groundbreaking research strictly defined the concept of poverty and broke the traditionally held view that poverty was the fault of the poor. Winston Churchill's interest in social reform grew after he digested the report and it was with Lloyd George in the 1905 liberal government that Churchill's social reform agenda grew and marked him out as a one nation conservative as he sought to bridge the gap between the two nations of rich and poor identified by Benjamin Disraeli in *Sybil*.

After reading *Poverty: A Study of Town Life* (1901) by Seebohm Rowntree, Churchill wrote to an official of the Midland Conservative Association in December 1901 stating how impressed he was by Rowntree's book and that "[he saw] little glory in an Empire which [could] rule the waves [but was] unable to flush its sewers" (Marshall and Porion: 2023, 81).

Churchill was an advocate of minimum levels of wages, insurance against sickness, unemployment benefits, and old age provision. For Churchill, "...social reform was an urgent matter and the only question by which parties [were] going to live in the future" (Addison:1993, 60). In December 1908, he wrote to Prime Minister Asquith, comparing what was happening in Germany and that despite the harder life, climate, and far less accumulated wealth, Germany was able to establish tolerable basic conditions for her people. Winston Churchill went on to explain that Germany was organised not only for war but for peace, whilst Britain was only organised for party politics. Churchill explained to the prime minister that whoever could apply the successful experiences of Germany into Great Britain, might not be supported at the polls, but he would leave a memorial that time would not deface (Churchill: 1969). The Liberal Prime Minister Herbert Henry Asquith (1908 - 1916) (who took Great Britain into the First World War) was at the start of his premiership in December 1908, when Churchill wrote to him, imploring him that the need for social reform was "urgent and the moment ripe".

Prime Minister Asquith agreed to adopt a German-style approach to state intervention and oversaw key measures like, labour exchanges and unemployment insurance which marked the beginning of the end of the Poor laws which were modernised in the 1920s, but it was after 1945 under the labour government of Clement Atlee, that the universal right to pensions, health care and unemployment benefits came into force.

The Chancellor of the Exchequer in the liberal government was Lloyd George, and from 1908, he worked with Winston Churchill as Home Secretary and President of the Board of trade. Together, they brought in William Beveridge, (the author of the 1942, report, *Social Insurance and Allied Services*, also known as the Beveridge Report), into the government and the board of Trade. With this momentum, the first thing that Churchill decided to implement was a system of labour exchanges.

For Churchill, one of the key challenges and obstacles to people finding employment was that people were unable to find out where jobs were, and employers looking for workers were unable to find where the workers were. Securing work was very difficult so the first thing that Churchill implemented was the system of labour exchanges to address the mismatch and the hit-and-miss nature of job search. Over time, labour exchanges became essential for deploying unemployment insurance / benefits.

The second element of Churchill's reform agenda was the passing of the Trade Boards Act of 1909 (later updated in 1918). The act made provision for the creation of boards that could set enforceable minimum wage criteria in certain trades/industries that were renowned for their long hours, poor sanitation, low wages, and where workers were unable to organise in trades unions due to the jobs being low-skilled. There were other industries and sectors where there was an oversupply of labour, with the resultant effect that wages were pushed down and the conditions prevented workers from being able to bargain collectively for high wages. Churchill's position was that the government would not fix wages, but they could be fixed and adjusted based on local and industry-specific conditions and assisted by statutory wage boards, which were composed of workers and employers with an impartial chair (Marshall and Porion: 2023, 83).

This is an example of the Germanisation that Hayek so feared. Lloyd George had visited Germany and seen the compulsory national insurance system implemented by the German Chancellor Otto von Bismarck. Lloyd George set about emulating it, and the Liberal government led by Henry Campbell-Bannerman and H. H. Asquith, with Chancellor David Lloyd George and Winston Churchill as the Home Secretary, enacted the National Insurance Act of 1911. Originally, this was a system of health insurance for industrial workers, but over time, this was the first system of insurance against illness and unemployment that the British working class had. The act provided the foundations of the modern welfare state and has been widely accepted as one of the most important measures of social reform ever to be carried out by Parliament (Marshall and Porion: 2023, 83).

The Unemployment Insurance Act was meant to provide support for people in the immediate post-war years when unemployment was low. However, after the war, unemployment increased, and in the inter-war years, unemployment increased further, putting a huge burden on the state to deal with large-scale unemployment and, in some cases, permanent unemployment.

As early as 1931, a Royal Commission said that the scheme was carrying a load that it was not designed to bear (Marshall and Porion: 2023, 86).

Churchill was at the forefront of a new consensus in Britain that saw the liberals, the conservatives - to a lesser degree - and a Labour government implement social reforms that all could benefit from. The social reforms that marked Churchill out as a One Nation Conservative were enacted after he had crossed to the Liberals in 1904 and while he sat as a member of the Liberal Cabinet after 1908. Churchill was indeed a One Nation Conservative who wasn't actually in the Conservative Party.

In December 1918, at a Chamber of Commerce luncheon in Dundee, Winston Churchill, as a member of the liberal party, discussed the state of the national finances and the World War I debt that Britain owed the United States. Churchill stated that the country needed to do something on a bigger scale to get out of debt. He argued for the public ownership of the railways.

> 'So long as the railways are in private hands, they may be used for immediate profit. In the hands of the state, however, it may be wise or expedient to run them at a loss if they develop industry [and] place the trader in close contact with his market, and stimulate development.
>
> You cannot organise the great questions of land settlement, new industries, and the extension of production unless the state has control of the means of transportation' (Chamber of Commerce 1918).

The *Ways and Communications Bill 1919*, (Paragraph a), permitted a continuation of the status quo, with control exercised by the Board of Trade through the Railway Executive, without the need to renew the warrant from the Secretary of State every week. Paragraph *b* of the bill, however, gave power to the Ministry to "take possession" after one month's notice of any of the other railways not already controlled, such as light railways and tramway railways not opened by local authorities. It gave the Ministry the right to exercise the same control that the government exercised over the railways during the war.

The country's 120 railway companies were making huge losses, and Andrew Bonar Law, leader of the Conservative Party and later prime minister (Oct 1922 - May 1923), was opposed to railway nationalisation, and under the Railways Act 1921, he removed the power to nationalise the railways and enshrined the grouping of rail companies into regional monopolies. *The Railways Act of 1921* was an attempt to halt the losses, to prevent internal competition and to ensure that the country was able to benefit from the efficient way that the government-controlled railways were run and managed during the first World War (1914-1918) and immediately after.

Winston Churchill became Conservative Prime Minister again: from 1940 - 1945 (defeated in 1945 by the Labour leader Clement Attlee) and between 1951 - 1955. Churchill led Britain into war from 1940 to 1945. Curiously, given his central role in the establishment of the welfare system as we know it, in his first election broadcast after 1945, Winston Churchill spoke of the dangers of planning an ideal society, stating that the government would need the powers of a Gestapo if it wanted to implement its plan (Shearmur: 2006). Clement Attlee criticised the speech, and by extension, he was indirectly criticising one of the main thrusts of Hayek's argument in *The Constitution of Liberty*. In 1951, Churchill became prime minister for the second time; this time Britain was not at war. During his second stint as prime minister, and despite the expectation that he would dismantle much of the welfare state provisions of Clement Atlee, Churchill preserved the welfare state measures enacted by Attlee's Labour government after 1945. The fact that he did not dismantle the very policies that he was personally instrumental in bringing in, but which were then enacted by a labour government, further solidifies Churchill's reputation as a One Nation Conservative

By 1946, in response to questions in the House of Commons on the King's speech, Winston Churchill resiled from advocating taking railways into state control explaining that nationalisation had failed, based on recent evidence. Winston Churchill explained that the government had placed Sir Eric Geddes in charge of the railways and had given him all the power of a state-aided nationalised industry; but rather than the service improving, over a four-year period, it worsened, it returned heavy losses to the shareholders, and Britain experienced "the worst railway strikes ever known except the one preceding the general strike" (Churchill: 1948; 241-42). Churchill had warned that the nationalisation of public services - or, as he put it - "the complete nationalisation of production, distribution and exchange would make it impossible for Britain to support a large part of its population". During his second premiership (1951 – 1955), with the exception of the steel and trucking industries, he did not engage in wide-scale denationalisation.

Without being directly influenced by Hayek, whom he only met once when he (Churchill), was drunk; Churchill had learned from experience and moved pragmatically away from advocating the state-control of industries to becoming a proponent of the free market. It is crucial to note that at the time when Churchill was advocating for state control, he and the liberal government realised that post-war, there needed to be a national effort to not only pay down the war debt to the USA but also to rebuild the economy of the United Kingdom. At this time, the government required that all those industries that had been sequestered during the war to support the production of war-related munitions, clothing, and other supplies be repurposed to their original focus, pooling their efforts in support of UK growth.

Between 1945 and 1951, Britain had a mixed economy of private and nationalised industries. Post-First World War, there were two key things that the government feared had the potential to threaten and act as a break on UK economic growth. The first was the monopoly control of the UK economy by private industry, and the second was the government's inability to control and utilise national utilities to benefit the whole nation.

In the 1930s, cartels and monopolies had formed in many industries. With the increased demand for iron and steel after World War 1, there was rapid growth and expansion of companies in critical sectors. The steel and iron industries in particular began to work together, forming agreements to control prices and distribution, which was particularly useful to them when the government subsidised them and when demand declined in the 1920s. The iron and steel industry cartelized and formed the British Iron and Steel Federation, which the British government reluctantly recognised because it needed them in the interwar years to deliver on its rearmament programme. With the high demand for iron and steel, the government established price controls on these industries to prevent exorbitant profiteering and wide-scale monopolisation. The banking sector was not immune from these practises and behaved in ways similar to cartels. For example, there were mergers that, whilst requiring the approval of the Treasury, were always approved and resulted in the appearance/creation of some of the largest banks (Barclays, Lloyds, Midland, National Provincial, and the London & Westminster bank) in the UK. Banks collectively increased loan rates after the end of World War I to their advantage (Braggion, Dwarkasing, and Moore: 2012; Capie and Billings: 2004). The government tried in 1919 but failed to pass the Joint Stock Banks Amalgamation Act. It was only after 1951 that the conservative government decentralised the industry, and in 1956, it passed the Restrictive Trade

Practises Act. Although it excluded banks and other monopolies that did not trade physical goods, it enforced competition by compelling companies involved in restrictive trading to be placed on a public register, and any changes to those agreements needed to be notified and appear on the register (Dennison: 1959).

The second key thing was the perceived need for nationalisation, as the government was unable to direct and utilise national resources and utilities to benefit the whole nation. The coal, rail, transport, electricity, and gas industries were taken into public ownership, and in 1951, Clement Atlee's Labour government nationalised the Iron and Steel Corporation of Great Britain (ISCGB). Although nationalisation was not traditional conservative policy, when the conservatives returned to office under Winston Churchill in 1951, he and they accepted, or at least, didn't seek to re-privatise these nationalised industries. In its 1974 election campaign, the conservatives again accepted the status quo and dismissed the possibility of large-scale privatisation except for the iron industry, which it had begun to privatise again in 1953 after Churchill replaced the ISCGB with the Iron and Steel Holdings Realisation Agency. The conservative government saw it as unfeasible to sell off all the nationalised industries, and some industries were regarded as natural monopolies and would thus need to remain under public control.

In the aftermath of the war, the competitive market had a minimal role, and the state was active and dominant in the planning and orchestration of the rejuvenation of the British economy. A formidable trades union movement grew in Britain due to the political and economic consensus around the need to increase public expenditure on welfare, maintain the public ownership of basic and monopoly services and industries, and the commitment to full employment. This approach, according to Keynes, was the correct role of the state during difficult times; but for Hayek, the state should not have been at the helm of orchestrating and planning the UK economy in this way.

Post-War Dis-Agreement

Britain had literally been through the wars. From 1939 to 1945, the country was governed by a coalition government led by Winston Churchill. The country had, and was still going through a difficult time with low productivity and was in need of a coherent economic plan for growth. There had not been a general election in Britain since 1935, and the British public wanted their politicians to head off the palpable sense of desperation felt by many Britons. The opportunity came at the 1945 general election, which ushered in a Labour government under Clement Atlee. Having won the 1945 general election, the labour government promised widescale social reform, which included establishing a welfare state with a national insurance system, so for the first time, citizens would have help with family income and health when times were hard. There was also reform, an expansion of social housing, and the nationalisation of key industries. Between 1945 and the late 1970s, there was general agreement on a range of core domestic policies that politicians believed would signal and usher in a better country and a better future. The principal tenets of this consensus included;

1. A commitment to full employment
2. Accepting the role and importance of trades unions in boosting the increase in economic activity,
3. A mixed economy of state-owned utilities - like gas, electricity, coal, rail – and private enterprise,
4. Agreement of the need for an effective welfare state.

These measures formed part of a cross-party agreement and were deemed necessary for the economic recovery and for rebuilding Britain after the devastation of the war years. Historians and political scientists have variously argued that this period of cross-party agreement formed a political and economic post-war consensus in British politics, which existed from 1945 and the end of World War II, to the late 1970s, when Edward Heath challenged, but failed to break the consensus mindset which had persisted. The full-blown emergence of Margaret Thatcher as conservative party leader and as prime minister was the death knell of that consensus.

For me, however, the post-war consensus actually emerged in a recognised form in May 1940 when Winston Churchill took office as prime minister and headed a coalition government that led Britain through the Second World War. Churchill's hunger for reform; his subsequent defection to the Liberals; his pioneering work on welfare (labour exchanges, national insurance); his defection back to the conservative party were central to the birth and the crystallisation of not only a post-war consensus that the 1945 Atlee labour government brought to fruition, but also the start of the one nation vision that the conservative party used masterfully to solidify its position as the natural party of government. The principal tenets of this consensus included the commitment to full employment, harnessing the benefits of a mixed economy, the active role of unions, and the establishment of a welfare state, along with a consensus on social justice and equality. Despite small divisions over Suez in 1956, the Labour Party's opposition to nuclear weapons and Britain's membership in the European Economic Community, there was a high level of agreement as to the means of achieving economic and social development.

Neither the 2020 COVID pandemic nor the 2008 banking crisis - which were both systemic national and international crises - were able to bring about the level of cross-party, cross-government, private, voluntary sector, and citizen consensus. Notwithstanding this, there were disagreements around the nature and role of the state – which is, after-all, the basis of this book.

The notion of there being a post-war consensus should be treated with some caution. Pimlott, in *Is the Postwar Consensus a Myth*? (1989), and Jessop, in *Thatcherism: A Tale of Two* Nations (1988), stated that the so-called consensus did not entail agreement between all major political parties on matters of political, social, or economic activity. For Jessop, any notion of a post-war consensus around the idea of a Keynesian-style welfare state was extremely 'limited by atlanticist foreign policy and financial policy and it was undertaken, not under the 'hegemony of the Labour Party or the working class but under the dominance of financial capital' (Jessop et al; 1988.9). In other words; for the conservative party and those on the political right, the aim of the post-war consensus was to make capitalism work. Within the Conservative camp, some emphasis was placed on the private sector and less on state intervention, while Labour's policy stance was a drive for nationalisation and higher public expenditure. However, I think it would be fair to accept that even though there were these differences; fundamentally there was agreement on the broad strategy of reducing welfare spending, reducing inflation, and the equal and opposite solution of committing to full employment.

Full Employment

In June 1944, Minister of Labour, Ernest Bevin, produced a White Paper on Employment (CMND 6527). This command paper committed future Labour and Conservative governments to the objective of achieving full employment. This was the first time that there was an official government document committing the government to achieving high and stable levels of employment as one of its primary responsibilities after the war (Hansard:

1944 v 401). The White Paper, however, made it clear that even if government intervention could ameliorate or even prevent long-lasting depressions, the government still could not implement a programme of full employment. What Bevin was successful in doing was demonstrating that there was a high level of agreement on the causes of unemployment, and the benefits of pursuing high levels of employment as an economic policy.

During the interwar years (1919-1938), the employment rate of people aged 16 and over averaged 64 percent. Between 1946 and 1970, the average employment rate was 73 percent. The lowest rates of employment occurred during the Great Depression, where employment fell to a low of 61 percent, followed by the early 1980s recession, where it rose to 66 percent (ONS: 2021).

Keynes had identified three types of unemployment. Frictional, voluntary, and involuntary. Frictional unemployment occurred when people left one job but would rarely be in another one quickly, or would not take the first job offered but would shop around, take a few days' additional holiday and they might have savings which meant that they didn't need to hasten their return to the work place. Voluntary unemployment occurred when a worker was unwilling or unable to accept a job - for whatever reason. Keynes described this as a demand issue where workers are able to choose. Involuntary unemployment is when a worker is unable to find work because of a supply issue or a deficiency in demand (Keynes: 2009, 7-9). For Keynes, the involuntary unemployed were those who were willing and able to work but who had been unemployed for over eight weeks. Keynes saw the only way to ensure the full employment of the 'involuntarily unemployed' was to advocate for an increased role for the state because, for him, the idea that free markets could balance themselves in a way that created profits while realising full employment was a delusion. Keynes argued that his model/theory of economic management reconciled the conflict between planning and freedom in the areas of politics and economics. Keynes argued that inadequate demand in consumption, investment, government purchases, and net exports led to inefficient macroeconomic outcomes like recessions, which could lead to periods of high unemployment. Additionally, inflation, where demand is too high, also had negative macroeconomic outcomes, denuding the real value of wages. To guard against prolonged high unemployment and to moderate the booms and busts, Keynes argued that state intervention was necessary in economic business cycle (Keynes: 2009).

Over time, the *New Right* had grown tired of the commitment to full employment due to its inflationary effects on an economy, and argued against it. Margaret Thatcher agreed, as outlined by Hayek, that a move to a more natural, market-directed level of employment was preferable to one dictated by those who wanted a managed economy. A market-directed approach, they thought, would consequently lessen the risk of high inflation.

Given the poor state of the British economy and the obvious need for government-led growth and investment, it was almost inevitable that the Keynesian doctrine would prevail over the competitive capitalism and monetarism of Friedman and the Hayekian free market. After all, the option of market-led growth was not only politically unpalatable given the impact of the cartels and monopolies that previously existed, but the economic depression showed that the classical economics of the market was not working as theorists had predicted it would. Keynesianism came along and seemed to lend itself quite amicably to both the Conservative and Labour Party governments. The fundamental argument of Keynes was that full employment was desirable and should be striven for because there was no necessary link between savings, investments, and consumption. For Keynes, the government's role was to stabilise economic activity. If demand was deficient and the national income and level of employment fell below reasonable levels, the Treasury should budget for a deficit and encourage state and private spending via tax cuts or reduced interest rates. If, however, demand was too high, it was the government's responsibility to budget for a surplus by reversing these measures.

Keynesianism underpinned the post-war consensus and gave credence to proactive state intervention as a safety net and as a mechanism to balance the economy, as opposed to a laissez-faire free market approach. Sir William Beveridge Review of Social Security (Social Insurance and Allied Services,1942 pp.6-7 Cmnd 6404) played a vital role in this agenda as it provided tangible activities and measurable outcomes that both politicians and citizens could see, and to a large degree, measure or assess. The key aim of Beveridge was to combat want and need, and to that end, he proposed that the separate schemes of pensions, unemployment, and sickness benefit should be consolidated into a universal national insurance scheme. One of the main propositions from Beveridge was that Social Security should be part of a comprehensive plan for welfare, and include a National Health Service and full employment. His report, although stressing the need for governmental help, had as its third guiding principle, the recommendation that individualism must be retained and that social security must be achieved by cooperation between the state and the individual, and the state should not stifle individual development or take away the responsibility of the individual to provide for the family.

Keynesianism and Beveridge set a new bar; together, they incorporated fairness; equality; the state's role as provider of essential goods; and the state as the mechanism for redistributing resources from the rich to the poor. Keynesianism and Beveridge marked the end of an era of hardship for British citizens and the beginnings of a new approach to serving the needs of the British public. In contrast, Hayekian economics of the free market was seen as too cold and detached, at a time when the country needed a European and US-style approach that was predicated on protecting citizens from hardship, and the potential ravishes of a market led economy with its propensity to seek profits at all costs.

Crisis in Confidence

With the steady erosion and collapse of the postwar consensus; from the 1970s onwards, there was a vacuum that the *New Right* began to fill. The emphasis on the free market, on competition, and on the retrenchment of the state, ensured that the control of the money supply was at the heart of this new doctrine as it set its face against the Keynesian economic strategy adopted after the Great Depression and the Second World War.

The consensus and the state interventionist approach began to wane even further when, in 1970, the Conservative Party, under Edward Heath, took power with a commitment to implementing radical free market economic policies. As time elapsed, the Heath government continued its commitment to maintaining a mixed economy and supporting the welfare state, which seemed to adhere much more to the post-war consensus than was initially assumed.

There are four key things that Edward Heath did that underscore this. In 1971, in order to prevent the sterling crisis from impeding his strategy for economic expansion, Heath abandoned the fixed exchange rate and floated the pound, thus reducing sterling's role as an international reserve currency. Floating the pound meant that the exchange rate was no longer set by the government but that it would fluctuate based on the market. This meant that the value of the pound could fall and rise quite considerably (Gamble: 1974, 121). Edward Heath's Chancellor, Anthony Barber, variously described as the worst Chancellor of the Exchequer in history – a title that may have passed to Kwasi Kwarteng - presided over a tax-cutting budget that led to a brief boom and announced spending cuts worth £1.1bn in his 1970 budget. In order to fund this, he withdrew subsidies from industry, cut spending on housing and welfare, and in the following year – 1971, he cut income tax and the top rate of tax. In addition to these measures, Barber supported the easing of credit controls and decided not to increase interest rates, which would have acted as a restraint on spending and caused the market to overheat. In addition to this blizzard of announcements and changes, Baber also announced reforms to corporation tax and the introduction of value-added tax (VAT) to replace sales taxes. As a direct result, Britain began to experience high inflation, high unemployment, and stagflation, where wages and prices spiralled and sterling was devalued. The incoming Labour government was forced to deal with the 1976 sterling crisis. The doctrine of free market economics was again discredited; once after the war as the United Kingdom sought to rebuild under a Keynesian economic consensus and now, after the disastrous budget of Anthony Barber.

Secondly, Edward Heath set about dismantling much of the apparatus of state economic intervention created during the interwar years, and in order to counter inflation, he moved away from price and income policies, dismantling the National Board for Prices and Incomes, which was created by Harold Wilson in 1965 to exercise wage-price controls (Gamble: 1974; Hunter,

1975; 67-84). Heath also dismantled the Industrial Reorganisation Corporation established in 1966 to promote the efficiency and international competitiveness of British industry; and did away with the system of investment grants.

Thirdly, the class character of Edward Heath's new fiscal policies was unmistakable, as the burden of taxation was substantially shifted away from companies and rich tax payers onto the working class (Leys: 1989). Indirect evidence of the balance shifting could be seen in the reduction in the subsidy given to council housing, replacing controlled rents with fair rents, which in effect led to an increase in rents under the new Housing Finance Act 1972.

The fourth key thing that Edward Heath did was that he began moves to limit the power of trades unions and began to implement the kind of union-controlling legislation that the Labour Prime Minister, Harold Wilson, had failed to implement. In 1969, Wilson proposed changes to the legal basis for industrial relations in his Industrial Relations White Paper *In Place of Strife* (Cmnd 3888) 1969. The TUC opposed the proposals, and the Wilson government recanted them, but they were never passed into law. It was, however, the Edward Heath government (1970-1974) that continued and pushed through the Industrial Relations Act in 1971. Heath had rejected the notion of compulsory wage control and believed that collective bargaining could be effective within the parameters of new labour laws. The Industrial Relations Act 1971 which Heath brought in, set about restricting the legal privileges of trades unions, and unsurprisingly, it was met with huge hostility from the unions (Moore: 2013). The act came into force in 1972 introducing punitive financial sanctions on registered unions whose membership took industrial action other than through prescribed procedures.

Under the act, unofficial and sympathy strikes became either illegal or vulnerable to civil law suits. The act imposed compulsory cooling off periods and strike ballots before strikes could be called; unions lost their immunity to civil actions from employers if they decided not to register under the act. Unsurprisingly, the labour movement was opposed to the 1971 Industrial Relations Act and saw it as a frontal attack on the ability of unions to express solidarity with fellow striking workers elsewhere. The Industrial Relations Act of 1971 was the prime cause of the eventual defeat of the Heath government. There were mass union protests against the legislation; coal miners and railway workers went on strike; there were electricity blackouts; and in order to conserve electricity, Edward Heath implemented a three-day week between January and March 1974.

The blatant and successful union show of strength against the Heath government demonstrated that when unions united, they were, at times, far stronger than the government. Confrontation between the government and unions increased, and relations were made worse because, internationally, the long economic boom or golden age, which began after World War II (Middleton: 2000 and Skidelsky: 2009), came to an end in 1970 as competition for manufactured goods became more intense and exports became increasingly harder to sell. This saw the simultaneous appearance in the economy of slow growth, high unemployment, stagnant wages, and rising prices. This anomaly; known as stagflation, was a phenomenon that economist's thought was impossible. Typically, when prices went up and wages went up, inflation rose. Due to a lack of investment, the government found itself forced to roll the state forward instead of rolling it back.

The stance conservative governments and proponents of the free market held was that competition was of paramount necessity because it dictated that weak companies would be weeded out of the market, and it meant that governments had no role to play in subsidising and artificially propping up failing enterprises. In 1971, having realised that the electorate was not ready to accept industrial recession, which would have been the consequences of a consistent application of free market doctrine, the Heath government dramatically intervened in the market and decided to rescue Rolls Royce by nationalising it. This was one of the Heath government's now-infamous U-turns, reverting to the essential strategies of the 1960s. Edward Heath had won the 1970 general election on a manifesto promising to cut public expenditure, limit immigration, resist union wage demands, halt the propping up of failing companies, and abandon the Wilson government's wage control policies. By 1972, he had turned on them all. After declaring the three-day week, Heath conceded to the National Union of Mineworkers and gave them a 27 percent wage increase, plus overtime, holidays, and pensions: With unemployment going over a million, he increased public spending dramatically. Heath was heavily criticised for these U-turns; however, if nothing else, his actions showed that a), he was a political pragmatist; b), at heart he was a product of the post-war consensus, which – even as a conservative, did not baulk at the state engaging where market failure was evident; and c), his attempts to steady the ship showed that the free market had no answer to inflation or stagnation. Maybe monetarism and fiscal policies such as the Medium-Term Financial Strategy (MTFS) - implemented by the Thatcher government in its first term, along with abandoning the post-war commitment to full or high employment as the goal of government, are the prime means for fighting inflation and growing the British economy.

In the run-up to the 1974 general election, Edward Heath and the conservative party campaigned with the slogan, 'Who rules Britain?". The unrest and industrial disputes demonstrated clearly that the conservative party/government were not in control. Despite the economic and political turmoil in the country, the Heath government was narrowly defeated by Harold Wilson, whose Labour Party won by a slim majority of only three seats.

Harold Wilson, who had previously been Labour prime minister between October 1964 and 1970 took Labour into power again (from 1974 -1976) on a manifesto that pledged that there would be a fundamental and irreversible shift in the balance of power and wealth in favour of the working class and their families (Sewell: 2003). The first task that Harold Wilson set himself was to repair the relationship with the unions: For Wilson, the unions were the cornerstone of reviving the British economy. In an attempt to arrive at a new price and incomes policy, a social contract was agreed upon with the Trades Union Congress, which fostered an understanding and a certain level of cooperation between the state, capital, and labour. The acceptance of price and incomes policies to control increases in prices and wage was socialist and went against the principles of the conservative party; however, the economic crisis was extreme, and as such, it required extreme temporary measures, which Her Majesty's official opposition – the conservative party, broadly accepted. Wilson was also cautious on the subject of nationalisation and only promised to nationalise the ailing industries of shipbuilding, aircraft, and docks. The miners' strike was settled; the rights of trades unions were restored by repealing the Industrial Relations Act 1971 and replacing it with the Trade Union and Labour Relations Act 1974, which itself was later repealed and replaced by the Trade Union and Labour Relations (Consolidation) Act 1992. With the passage of time, memories faded, and it was barely noticed that this latter act contained many similar provisions outlined in the initial Industrial Relations Act. This new 1974 Act contained more complex, more restrictive, and – to a degree – more ambiguous provisions around the legal status and functioning of trades unions. What was also clear was that the Wilson government was concerned about the plight of the working class, and job security was set to be improved by the other element of the social contract, the Employment Protection Act 1975 which also established the Advisory, Conciliation, and Arbitration Service (ACAS). Sir Alan Bullock was asked to chair what became the Bullock Commission to review labour relations, corporate governance, and put forward recommendations for industrial democracy. This was stakeholder capitalism. Big business and the political right hated the recommendations, and there was no political unity amongst unions. With unions like the TGWU and – reluctantly, the – TUC supporting it, AUEW felt that having a 50:50 split of shareholder and employee votes electing members to a single-tier unitary board and having members contribute to management decisions would compromise the voice of the unions (Lea and Ackers: (2010). In the end, the commission was abandoned, and its recommendations fell away due to other political issues becoming more urgent.

The first Wilson government of 1964 undertook significant social reform, abolishing capital punishment, relaxing divorce laws, limiting immigration, liberalising birth control and abortion laws, and partially decriminalising male homosexuality in England and Wales. Another sign of the Wilson government's innovation and forward thinking was that the government realised that most of the working-class population did not have bank accounts, so in 1968, his government created the publicly owned 'people's bank' called the National Giro, then it became Girobank PLC, which was run by the post office and continued until 2003. His government expanded the creation of new universities. After losing the 1970 general election to Edward Heath, the second Labour government (1974-1979) (Harold Wilson was prime minister from 1974-76 and James Callaghan took over as prime minister from 1976–1979), focused on public ownership and the referendum on Britain's membership in the European Community (EC). Despite the difficult economic climate, the government was committed to increasing spending on education, health, and housing. To fund this increased spending, the Wilson government reversed the conservative government's reduction in the higher rate tax, which had been cut from 90 percent to 75 percent. In his first budget, Chancellor Denis Healy increased this to 83 percent, along with increasing the top rate of tax on investment income to 98 percent.

Labour's second term in office was at a time of economic crisis. In Britain, the rate of inflation rose from 10.2 percent in 1973 to 24.6 percent in 1975 and rose to 25 percent in 1975. The balance of payments deteriorated from a deficit of £923 million in 1973 to £3,565 million in 1974. Unemployment in 1974 was half a million and reached one million in mid-1975 and 1.6 million in 1976. Britain had a crisis in sterling in 1976 due to high inflation, a deteriorating balance of payments deficit, a public spending deficit, and the effects of the 1973 oil crisis. In order to maintain the value of Sterling The Prime Minister, James Callahan, requested $3.9 billion from the International Monetary Fund, of which $1.95 billion was drawn down and was repaid by the general election in 1979.

James Callaghan had served as Chancellor of the Exchequer in the first Labour government of Harold Wilson; he then served as Home Secretary in Harold Wilson's second government in 1974 and then became Prime Minister from 1976 to 1979.

During James Callaghan's premiership, he oversaw the passage of unpopular cuts in government spending, was consequently assailed by trades unions, and was unable to halt their demands for wage increases. The patience of the workers had by now grown thin, and the fragile political and economic balance lay in their hands. In 1978, the Trades Union Congress refused labour prime minister James Callaghan's request for a fourth year of wage restraints. A series of large-scale strikes ensued during one of the coldest winters in living memory: this became known as the Winter of Discontent, when snow lay uncleared, bins unemptied, and schools closed. Supported by the Scottish National Party, a motion of no confidence was moved against the government by Mrs Thatcher. During the 1979 election campaign, Mrs Thatcher attacked the unions and declared as totally false, Labour's claim that it was the only party that unions would listen to. This was in contrast to a statement she had made some years earlier, during the 1972 rail dispute, when she asserted that the real battle was and should be presented [as being] between unions and the people's (Moore: 2013. 236, 238). Margaret Thatcher promised to reduce state spending, cut income tax, and reduce immigration. Labour lost that election. This was the first time that a vote of no confidence had brought down a government since the defeat of the Labour minority government led by Ramsay MacDonald in 1924.

CHAPTER 3

Enoch Powell, Thatcherism and the New Right

There were examples of *New Right* politics emerging in many countries. In the United Kingdom, the *New Right* was personified by Margaret Thatcher, and in the United States of America, Ronald Reagan was the embodiment of *New Right* economic and political thinking. The intellectual underpinnings for the *New Right* came from Friedrich Von Hayek of the 'Austrian School' of Economics and Milton Friedman of the 'Chicago School' ((University of Chicago). Hayek feared creeping statism, coercion, and the state's encroachment into people's lives. Friedman, who became the economic adviser to US President Ronald Reagan, argued that the responsibility of the government was to ensure sound currency by controlling the supply of money in the economy. Friedman was the father of monetarism. One of the distinctive aspects of the *New Right* economic model was its belief that the best way of tackling inflation was through the adoption of 'supply-side economics' which called for lower taxes, free trade, and deregulation.

Bodies like the Institute of Economic Affairs, founded in 1955 and heavily influenced by Hayek, and the Centre for Policy Studies (CPS) in 1974, co-founded by her mentors Sir Keith Joseph, Alfred Sherman, and herself, set about undermining the Keynesian economic strategy. Another of the influences on Margaret Thatcher was Enoch Powell, who, as a member of the One Nation Group of Conservatives, critiqued the statist postwar settlement. Enoch Powell disliked the post-war settlement, and he saw that the modern state had produced a generation that saw the government as its servant, and the government's role was to provide for people's wants and needs, which they demanded as rights. Powell was initially an ardent believer in free trade and saw British membership in the Common Market as an attack on Parliamentary sovereignty and as anti-free trade. However, in the 1960s, realising Britain's diminishing position as an imperial power; the ineffectiveness of the Commonwealth to project British influence; and his dismissal of the UK-USA special relationship, he recanted and supported Britain's applications to join the Common Market. After his infamous 1968 River Tiber speech, he returned to his former anti-European Economic Community position. Very little is made of the importance of Enoch Powel in the development of the *New Right* and of Thatcherism. Powell was well aware of the contradictions of the *New Right* Group in relation to their support for marketisation and a free economy while simultaneously favouring strong government and championing competition while retaining nationalisation. In addition, there was support for equality of opportunity and a belief in incentives and rewards. Part of the *New Right* agenda was to see a reduction in welfare and state expenditure, but yet, they depended on the votes of those most reliant on that spending increasing (Longden: 1952, 1). Powell had been a major influence in the conservative party on market economics, but later, it was his views on immigration that diminished his standing. In order to address these contradictions, Powell set up a polarised position between the individual, the collective, the state, and the free market. In so doing, he laid the groundwork for the *New Right* to be the midwife of Thatcherism. In fact, there was evidence that the electorate was to the right of the main political parties on issues like immigration, law and order, schools, capital punishment, and trades unions, but that it was the parliamentary elite who set and controlled the policy agenda (Boyson: 1978). Populists like Enoch Powell had argued that on issues like immigration, the European Community, and Ulster's relationship to Ireland, a minority was manipulating the majority and expecting the majority to distrust what they were seeing themselves. For Enoch Powell, the way to address this was to have a right-wing conservative leader who was willing to espouse policies that challenged the prevailing view and promoted the view and opinions of the silent minority (Wood: 1970, 108). The use of the term *New Right* is, and can be contested because it does not mean that all individuals on the right were right-wing in all their machinations, beliefs, and admonitions. It is important to note that Powell was both a liberal in that he embraced free market economics; he voted against the restoration of capital punishment; he co-sponsored a parliamentary bill to legalise homosexuality between consenting adults; but he was also illiberal on immigration. There was also the Tory strand of *New Right* conservatives who, as libertarians, believed in the rights of the individual, free markets, monetarism, and competitive capitalism, while there were those who believed in the authority of the state; were less liberal; sided with stronger law enforcement measures; saw public benefit as being good, and wanted a return to core values associated with national identity and patriotism.

The *New Right* theory argued that a smaller 'neoliberal state was best placed to realise increased economic output and that through trickle-down economics, the poorest in society would benefit as wealth would spread downwards from the successful and the wealthy to the rest of society (Plant: 2009). The *New Right* was never about fairness and equality; it was about competition and the free market, and therefore inequality was an expected and desirable natural outcome because inequality could be a catalyst for innovation and growth.

> 'When the Conservative government comes to power, many trade unions will have put it there. Millions of them vote for us in every election. Go out and join in the work of your

unions; go to the meetings; stay to the end; and learn the union rules. Remember that if parliamentary democracy dies, free trade unions die with it'
(Thatcher: 1989, 27).

From the moment she became the leader of the Conservative Party in February 1975, Mrs Thatcher made it clear that her determination was to create the conditions for the economic revival that Britain so desperately needed. The focus of Mrs Thatcher and the Conservatives was purely on economic growth. Economic growth was seen as the sole tool for creating growth and prosperity. In contrast, it was clear that the Harold Wilson government, while striving to stabilise the economy after the disastrous Barber Boom, realised that sustained growth required a strong quadripartite of political, social, legislative, and economic reform. Wilson succeeded in terms of many aspects of social and legislative reform: Tony Blair and Gordon Brown succeeded primarily legislatively, with changes such as independence of the Bank of England, devolved government, the minimum wage, and negotiated peace in Northern Ireland. Britain's post-war decline was deep and complex, and its roots were so broad that simply changing the party in power would not sufficiently address and solve our primary economic problems. As the leader of Her Majesty's official opposition, from 1975 on, Mrs Thatcher worked on a detailed agenda of radical change that she hoped would break the stagnant and inflationary climate that existed in British politics.

The post-war consensus of securing high or full employment was discarded amid fears that this would result in running the economy at its maximum capacity. In order to do this, the conservative party concluded that consequently it needed to reduce the strength and power of trades unions. Government retrenchment was also required in other areas, and there was an overall emphasis on rejecting state help in health, education, and welfare towards private provision, which opposition political parties and third-sector organisations argued would create two nations, greatly benefiting some while being detrimental to others. The conservative Party and – later, – government believed that the period of the last labour government was an example of state overreach, an overbearing level of state control that resulted in Britain having to go to the International Monetary Fund (IMF) for £4,000.000,000 (which incidentally, Britain did not fully draw down on). Margaret Thatcher declared that the state was overgrown, overreaching, and a parasitic obstacle to economic recovery. In order to stimulate growth, she aimed to cut income tax as well as state spending, particularly on those who were deemed to be scrounging off the state. The social contract had failed, and the British public needed a change of direction.

Mrs Thatcher had adopted and subscribed to the individualistic, anti-state, anti-union, and anti-egalitarian views of her party's right wing. She adopted the social market and monetarist economic doctrines, to which her friend Sir Keith Joseph had recently converted.

A Programme of Change

In her first address to the Institute of Social Economic Studies as leader of the Conservative Party in 1975, Mrs Thatcher expounded many of the ideas and policies that she believed, when put into practice, would create the basis for the economic revival of Britain. The themes and direction of travel in this speech mirror, in many important aspects, Hayek's, *The Constitution of Liberty*; and Milton Friedman's *Capitalism and Freedom*. In retrospect, it was clearly obvious; the evidence base that Mrs Thatcher drew on and the conclusions that she arrived at would inexorably lead her through a period of adopting monetarism to being an unabashed exponent and proponent of the free market approach to economics and government.

In her speech (at the Institute of Social Economic Studies) entitled *Let our children grow tall,* Mrs Thatcher drew on evidence from the Royal Commission on the Distribution of Income and Wealth (1974) - which had been set up by the previous Labour government and chaired by Lord Diamond, to explore and reject the view that despite welfare provisions, very little had changed and people in Britain continued to feel that there was huge disparity and an unequal distribution of income and wealth. The Diamond Commission reported that the share of taxable income of the poor had not increased; that the poor were much better off than at any time; that there was a tendency to accumulate wealth amongst lower income groups, hitherto unaccustomed to doing so (Diamond Commission: 1974,249-250). Mrs Thatcher noted that tax-free benefits in cash were available, and she brushed aside the preponderance of myths about inequality as untrue. For Mrs Thatcher, the reality was that the rich were getting poorer and the poor were getting richer due to market forces and the actions of the government through the tax system.

The Diamond Commission stated that the wide availability of pensions, increased home ownership, and the influence of trades unions in keeping income inequality down were crucial to understanding that there was a more equal distribution of wealth in the post-war period. Mrs Thatcher, like Hayek, believed that it was erroneous to think that taking wealth from the rich would make a significant impact or difference to the wealth of the bulk of the population; neither would be taxing the rich more heavily to pay for much more government spending.

Mrs Thatcher used the labour government's Diamond Commission to validate her plan and future policies on inequality, emphasising that even the Commission did not find evidence of widespread resentment over injustice in society. Additionally, there was no enthusiasm for eliminating what little injustice existed, and although a possible reason why people might have felt impelled to fight inequality was due to a simplistic desire to help their fellow man. In reality, '[fighting for inequality and injustice] seems to be due to a combination of envy and bourgeoise guilt, which is the sense of guilt and criticism that affects not only the very rich but also the poor, who were looking the other way at those poorer than themselves. The egalitarian who resents the gap between himself and those who are better off is envious, while conveniently forgetting their own obligations to those poorer than themselves' (Thatcher: 1975a). It is undoubtedly the case that she saw the expansion of the functions of the state and the pursuit of equality as causing damage to the economy, and although she did not see it as the sole cause of Britain being described as the 'sick man of Europe', the British sickness, Mrs Thatcher saw it as a major contributor.

Like Hayek, Mrs Thatcher saw the promotion of equality as undesirable because, in order to achieve equality, the extension of the welfare state and state control over people's lives were required. Extending the role and influence of the state was undesirable for individuals and the economy as a whole. Politically, she also disagreed with the idea that extending the role of the state to correct inequality would also strengthen the political and social framework necessary if political freedom and other values associated with democracy were to be preserved. Or, to put it another way; extending the role of the state to correct inequality would not strengthen British values and British democracy.

Mrs Thatcher accepted that in the beginning, much concern about injustice and inequality was genuine; however, as time progressed, more and more groups with grievances and common interests combined to pressure politicians and institutions for redress and justice. They are assisted in this by the growing scope for exploiting grievances. Many of these groups have little or no connection with political parties and often cannot find any natural niche in our political institutions.

In these circumstances, she says that the government finds itself under pressure, firstly, to respond to pressure groups outside parliament and the democratic framework, and secondly, to react to pressure arising in its attempt to resolve the apparent injustices. Often the correct channels are discredited before they are given a chance to work, or the authorities are induced, sometimes by threat of force, to alter the decisions or change the law retrospectively. Before too long, the same tactics will be used by other groups. Too often, direct action is buoyed up and stimulated by every topic of fairness or equality. There is little or no consideration of the consequences that the rest of society must bear. Rarely, if ever, do people notice that by giving into such pressures, a government is endorsing principles and creating precedents, which would be quite disastrous if applied generally.

In her speech, Mrs Thatcher said one of the foundations of modern democracy and the reason for its success was the growing impatience with the state of our societies. There had also been a recognition that much of the misery inflicted by nature on man, or by man towards himself, was avoidable and should be avoided. This has brought with it the naïve belief and expectation that there are few social ills that cannot be remediated or mitigated by the state. One can easily argue that the state must provide a service to all those in need: however, given one's commitment to the sanctity of life, it is easy to appear callous and brutal when speaking about the limited availability of resources and the cost of saving a life. It is easy to see how the evolution of expectations can lose touch with the real world. Human institutions are imperfect, and as such, they cannot iron out all the wrinkles in human character, the strictures of time, the laws of nature, or abolish scarcity. Hayek, writing about labour unions, noted the failure of the state's legislative and executive authorities to adequately control them by consistently applying the rule of law (Hayek:1982,66,55,122,143). Hayek stated that any return to the former principles of the rule of law had been blocked by the argument that the clock could not be turned back, along with ideas that saw human institutions as imperfect. For Hayek, these views harboured a fatalistic belief that we cannot learn from our mistakes, which for him was the most abject admission that we are incapable of using our intelligence (Hayek: 1960, 403).

Hayek demonstrated the second problematic aspect of equality and inequality by referring to two individuals both earning the same wages. Person One saves a lot of money, while Person Two spends their money. When both individuals retire; Person One will be wealthier than Person Two. This, Hayek argues, is a classic case of economic inequality, but it is not a classic case of unfairness or injustice. Equally, he mused; suppose that two individuals have the same intelligence, but that Person One goes to college, works hard, and ends with a high salary. Person Two chose to leave school and coast through life on a modest wage. Here again, there will be inequality in outcomes, but not in the gap between the two individuals. Hayek then argues that an egalitarian might ask for a share of the savings or as much pay as Person Two because of an apparent unfair situation. To do this, however, is to ignore the fact that society is a growing organism, constantly changing, and justice itself would become meaningless if each citizen determined for themselves what is fair.

Mrs Thatcher believed that the pursuit of equality was a mirage and that what was more desirable was the pursuit of equality of opportunity, which meant nothing unless it also meant the opportunity to be unequal and different.

What Mrs Thatcher seemed to be arguing for was a free society, not only because it guaranteed our liberties, but also because, like Hayek, she saw it as the best way of creating wealth and prosperity for the whole country and for providing better resources for those in need (Thatcher: 1975). Upon taking office, Mrs Thatcher argued that the Labour government's attack on private enterprise and their collectivist mindset had made it certain that there was nothing available for improvements in social services over the next few years (ibid). The aim of her conservative administration was to get private enterprise back on the road to recovery, not merely to give people more of their own money to spend, but to have more money to help the sick (ibid). The best way to achieve this was through profits, which in-turn would lead to high investment, well-paid jobs, and a better standard of living in the future. The *New Right* thinking and approach personified by Mrs Thatcher was that the government had to learn to leave companies with enough of their own profits to produce goods and profits for tomorrow (ibid). Here lies the obligation of the government to create the framework within which talent can be produced.

Mrs Thatcher argued that the socialist policies of the Labour Party were a local version of an international creed and that although socialists had an earnest desire for social justice, they had mistakenly elevated the state and changed its purpose into being an instrument of social regeneration. Just as Keynes and neo-Keynesians had done, they were relegating the role of the individual in their pursuit of economic stability and prosperity (Thatcher: 1979). In her speech to the Conservative conference in Blackpool in October 1975, Margaret Thatcher argued that the milder advocates of socialism were equally unconvincing in their view of human nature and that economic problems had deeper roots in human nature and did not start with economics. The expansion of state activity had occurred under two falsehoods: firstly, that nationalisation was justifiable because it made economic power more accountable, and secondly, that state planning could point to better ways forward than through free enterprise (Thatcher: 1975c).

It was the duty of government, whether Conservative or Labour, to give effective support to those in need; however, where the Conservative party and government differed from a Labour party and government was that the conservatives under Mrs Thatcher had little confidence in the exclusive capacity of the state to reduce suffering and promote well-being (Thatcher: 1979). There is no adequate substitute for genuine caring for one another on the part of families and friends—institutional charity would never be enough – but Mrs Thatcher insisted that the country could not afford to have a welfare system, which eroded individual and family responsibility (Ibid). She believed that the move towards collectivism had been too strong because it foisted the responsibility onto the state to provide for the education and health of the family.

The real-world economic impact was that when the government expanded its commitments and extended its activities, it caused wage earners to push against the subsequent rise in the tax burden, which then led to higher wages, lower profits, lower corporate taxes, and ultimately slow growth. The government is then deterred from raising taxes in line with its actual and future spending, which leaves a growing budget deficit as expenditure exceeds revenue and the government is forced to either borrow or print more money. Either of these actions devalues cash and savings. Along with this, the competition for labour and the switch from an industrial to a service economy as wealth increases will affect the pattern of employment and competition for labour between the private and public sectors. These factors all combine to create subtle distortions of the market that are not immediately felt.

Mrs Thatcher wanted to urgently roll back the state in order to reduce inflation and establish price stability, without which, - it was widely accepted, the supply side of the economy could not be improved. She set about seeking to establish a balance between the spheres of the public and private through monetary control. Incomes policies had been rejected, partly due to their demonstrable ineffectiveness and also because control over incomes was incompatible with supply-side performance. In her *Let the Children Grow Tall* speech, she argued that due to market forces and redistributive taxation, not only were the rich getting poorer and the poor richer, but taking more money from the rich or taxing them more would not make the majority of the population better off (Thatcher:1975).

Mrs Thatcher was a staunch believer in Adam Smith's teachings about the virtues of free markets and the inefficiency of government intervention that socialists made so much of. Similar to Hayek, in order to demonstrate her point about the imposition of the state on growth and taxation, she outlined an example of a man and wife with two children living on average industrial earnings. Since 1963, the state has increased its take from the average salary from 5 percent to 25 percent. The worker demands more wages to replace what has been taken away in tax. His call for higher wages has led to an acceleration of costs and prices since the mid-1950s, when the rate of inflation was 2 percent per annum, unlike today (1975) when it was 25 percent. The call for increased pay is aligned with the call for increased growth, but when there is no increase in growth but a growth in expenditure, it is sometimes financed by inflationary policies and puts the government budget under pressure (Thatcher: 1975).

The thinking behind the *New Right* was that growth and confidence would be stunted if people believed that the state owed them a living. The only way to ensure success was to encourage the workings of the market economy. In a free society, the role of the government is to ensure the maintenance of social cohesion through the support of established customs and traditions (Thatcher: 1979). Governments can animate industry but should not seek to sustain it. They should seek to purify the stagnant and corrupt parts of the economy and correct irregular ties in the market, but not seek to regulate the market (Thatcher: 1979). The government is also there to foster the new freedom by establishing sound money to squeeze out inflation. Much of this emphasis away from fiscal to monetary policy was experiential knowledge from history and was influenced by developments in economic theory.

In 1979, when Mrs Thatcher took office, her administration's approach to government spending and to the role of government was heavily influenced by the fact that Britain had previously approached the International Monetary Fund (IMF) and the Thatcher government needed to convince the IMF and international markets that Britain wasn't the sick man of Europe but that it had a plan to drive growth. It was therefore hardly surprising that her approach to the welfare state and wider public expenditure was informed and determined by her view that welfare provision and workers were in-part responsible for the high inflation and lack of growth. She set about holding down public expenditure and differentiated herself from previous labour administrations by challenging workers and the unions.

The attack of Thatcherites and the *New Right* on trades unions – and by extension, workers – found some of its theoretical justifications in Hayek's view that trade unions appeared to form monopolies in labour markets, which was antithetical to individual liberty-free markets. Hayek objected to collective action against employers, but he conceded that in a free society there should be no restrictions on the formation of trades unions. In this regard, the Employment Acts of 1980, 1982, 1988 and 1990 were examples of the Thatcherite agenda aligning with Hayek's view of monopoly trades unions.

In a speech at the Conservative Conference in Blackpool on October 12, 1979, Mrs Thatcher looked at the winter of discontent and said that unions did terrible damage to the industries that their members depended on. The key to economic rejuvenation did not come from awarding higher pay but from producing high output. The unions were winning pay awards that they did not deserve and that the country could not afford. The only lesson the Union seemed to be learning was that the military paid higher wages. According to Mrs Thatcher, what the government needed to do was make essential changes in the law and industrial relations and that what it could do, was stop the unions from coercing their members. The 1980 Employment Act diminished the potential effectiveness of collective action, attacked the closed shop by specifying that it must be periodically re-balloted, and also made unions liable for damage in the event of support for certain secondary actions. This was seen by the unions as an attempt to roll back the advance they had made over the years, and their resentment took the form of strikes, of which the coal miners were the most significant. With the government's success in beating the miners and their banning of unions at GCHQ, the power of the trades unions had seriously diminished. They no longer had the power to coerce.

In the run-up to the 1979 general election, the conservative party manifesto contained very little detail, but there were specific commitments to the welfare state. For example, nestled within the manifesto, was the commitment to support family life by helping people to become home-owners, raising the standards in education, concentrating welfare services on supporting the elderly, the sick, the disabled and those in real need. The manifesto also expressed that it was not the intention of a conservative government '...*to reduce spending on the Health Service; Indeed, we intend to make better use of the resources available. So, we will simplify and decentralise the service and cut back bureaucracy.*' Additionally,

> '... [we will not] discourage people from doing more for themselves. We shall therefore allow pay-beds to be provided where there is a demand for them; end Labour's vendetta against the private health sector; and restore tax relief on employer-employee medical insurance schemes' (Conservative Party Manifesto: 1979).

In an indication of the battles to come with the unions and with working people, the manifesto said that *'Too much emphasis has been placed on attempts to preserve existing jobs. We need to concentrate more on the creation of conditions in which new, more modern, more secure, and better-paid jobs come into existence. This is the best way of helping the unemployed and those threatened with the loss of their jobs in the*' (Conservative Party Manifesto: 1979) Overall, the manifesto captured the national feeling that things needed to change, and the conservative party's five main tasks were accepted by the electorate.

Five tasks

1. Controlling inflation, rebalancing the rights and duties of trade union power
2. The restoration of incentives meant that hard work and success were rewarded
3. Upholding parliament and the rule of law
4. Supporting family life through the more efficient provision of welfare services
5. Strengthening Britain's defence

In order to control inflation, the Thatcher government intended to operate with strict control over the supply of money, reduce government borrowing, and cut public spending. Her government also committed to selling shares in recently nationalised aerospace, shipbuilding, and national freight and promised to reduce the top rate of income tax to the European average of 60 percent and take lower-income earners out of taxation.

What emerged from this was a three-tiered approach, as set out in January 1983 in a Bow Group lecture given by Norman Fowler, the then Social Services Secretary. The first tier was that the proper starting point for the consideration of social policy was the economy. The second tier was anchored in the approach that the government should get the best possible value for the amount of money that the taxpayer provided, and thirdly, not everything can or should be done by the state.

It was evident to me that even among those who supported the welfare state, there was concern about the state's growing size and its drain on the public purse. With predictable inevitability, the welfare state was the target for the conservative party and the conservative right wing because the state was seen as the primary cause of higher taxes; it contributed significantly to budget deficits; and thirdly, if not handled carefully – which conservatives believed it wasn't – the state could unintentionally act as a further disincentive – along with low wages and high taxes—to work, rendering British workers work shy. There was also growing concern from the *New Right* and Thatcherites that increasing the reach of the state into the lives of citizens would foist additional responsibility and culpability on the state when things went wrong. This, in-turn, could encourage governments or the government to be soft on crime, strikes, and overall fecklessness. Additionally, there was the old class-based fear that the welfare state was potentially being used as the instrument of the left to engage in social reforms and the redistribution of wealth to the undeserving and the feckless.

At its creation, it was thought that the nation's demand for the services of the NHS would decline as health and lifespan improved as a result of better food, improved hygiene; sanitation; urban planning; advances in medical and social sciences, and as illnesses became more curable. In fact, demand for the NHS soared, in part due to the increase in the number of elderly citizens; increased lifespan; improvements in technology and drugs, which cumulatively resulted in people living longer and being treated for ailments that they would previously have succumbed to.

The Conservative government argued that increasing the take-up of private healthcare was the most effective means of alleviating pressure on the NHS. During the 1983 election campaign, Mrs Thatcher said that the National Health Service was safe in their hands and that it would not be the object of radical change. In January 1988, she announced a prime ministerial review of the service, which she personally chaired, accompanied by Kenneth Clarke and David Miller from Health, John Major from the Treasury, Malcolm Rifkind, and Peter

Walker from the Welsh and Scottish offices. In the following year, 1989, the White Paper *Working for Patients* was published. Under the commitment to give patients better healthcare and greater choice, its main recommendations were that hospitals and general practitioners were given finite budgets out of which patient care could be funded; that NHS hospital trusts be set up to run larger hospitals independently of the Health Service Administration (an opt out scheme); an internal market split between the purchaser and the provider would be developed whereby services could be bought from one NHS institution by another; there was a call for the exclusion of local authority representatives from the NHS management and the breakup of the Department of Health into a policy board and a management executive focused on the day-to-day running of the service.

Who could argue with a commitment to give patients better healthcare and greater choice, that money would follow the patient across administrative boundaries, that there would be rigorous audits of service quality; increases in the number of consultants, and the introduction of subsidiarity, where decisions and powers would be taken at the local level away from Whitehall?

For good or ill, the changes that were announced and subsequently implemented changed forever, the nature and the way that the social contract between the state and the citizen was structured and delivered. The attempt at a clean break from the post-war settlement and the move to adopt Friedman's monetarism and Hayek's liberty and free market principles was a necessary change. However, what was problematic and contentious was the speed at which the changes were brought about, the populism and the polarisation of the debate, that the private sector was good and the public sector being bad;

workers being seen as a drain on growth rather than integral to growth; capital, markets, and individualism being seen as good but collectivism as bad and costly. These polarised positions persist to this day, and Hayek; in equating collectivism and socialism with fascism, bears significant responsibility for this.

One of the most significant changes in the frontier between the public, i.e., state-run, managed, regulated, and controlled services along socialist or collectivist lines, and the private, i.e., privately run, privately managed, light touch regulation, competitive, and open to the free market, occurred in housing. The Thatcher government, on coming to power, proposed a sharp fall in expenditure on both new housing and housing subsidies, prompting the Environment Committee of the Commons to note in 1980 that the suggested strategy of reducing public expenditure relied principally on the achievement of the planned reduction in housing expenditure. New public sector house completions fell significantly from 1979 to 1982, leaving them at their lowest since the 1920s. During the same period, council rents more than doubled in cash terms as subsidies from the central government and from rate funds were cut. In 1981, outraged by this, the MP for Manchester, Ardwick; Gerald Kaufman, begged to move that the House condemn Her Majesty's Government for more than doubling council house rents since it came to power. When the government came into office in May 1979, the average council house rent was £6.40 a week. By April 1981, rents had risen to £11.39, which was an increase of 78 percent. Furthermore, the Chancellor of the Exchequer informed the House that in the coming financial year rents would increase to £13.59 a week – which was an increase - since the government came to power (HC: 1981).

One of the aims of the Thatcher administration was to introduce local authorities to market forces by requiring them to be self-financing and profit-making, thereby reducing the financial burden on the Treasury. As the Treasury and state began to roll back, a minimalist state was predicated on the rolling forward and – where possible – the maximisation of the private sector as the main provider of services like housing, health, etc., while the public sector would remain in the background as a safety net. The balance and the relationship between the public and the private began to alter as council rents increased, but the additional rent increase was excluded from the housing subsidy, putting the onus either on renters to pay more or on councils to absorb the losses. In addition, as a result of the 1980 Housing Act, council tenants who had lived in their homes for at least three years were notified that if they wanted to purchase their homes, they would receive a discount of 33 percent of the market price and 44 percent for a flat. For those tenants who had lived in their properties for over 20 years, they received a 50 percent discount. The results were quite dramatic, and circa 630,000 houses and flats and 40,000 housing association properties were sold between 1979 and 1983 (Hansard:1983, Vol 51). The social impact of this was stark as council estates became more ethnically and socially diverse. The new owners took pride in their homes, and the homes that were bought were distinctive because they invariably had new, improved double-glazed windows and neo-Georgian front doors. This was redistribution, and it exemplified the value of individual self-reliance and responsibility that Mrs Thatcher spoke so often about.

The sale of council homes was not only a skilful political move, but it captured a widespread and understandable desire for home ownership, and at the time, it challenged the traditional paternalistic idea of many local authorities, which had always advocated renting. The individuals who bought their homes would, in time, build up capital on a scale never seen before by manual workers and their families. This newly found wealth would be passed on to their children, who, in time, would also own their own homes, broadening the range of those in the community who owned assets as opposed to just earning income. For those families who could not buy their own homes; there was a widening of the social and economic divide between the middle class, the newly affluent working class, and the lower-paid and disadvantaged working class.

Monetarism & Privatisation

Was Margaret Thatcher a conservative? Conservatives were paternal, traditionalists; believing in a strong state; the rule of law; strong Christian and moral values, as personified by Benjamin Disraeli's and the One Nation Conservatism. Margaret Thatcher believed more in lowering taxes, sound money, a strong government, and rolling back the role of government where it was not needed. It therefore seemed to me that the Conservative Party was closer to her way of thinking than any other political party, and as such, her leap to monetarism was easier within these confines. However, for those on the right of the Conservative party – including some in her cabinet – it took time for them to agree with her brand of monetarism, and they were not converted to it based on economic evidence alone. With the support and knowledge of the works of Milton Friedman and her Chief Economic Adviser, Professor Sir Alan Walters, and with her interests in the works of Hayek, Mrs Thatcher won over the cabinet and the wider Conservative party. Mrs Thatcher explained that the advantage that she had over her contemporaries in politics was that they had to be persuaded of the theoretical advantages of monetarism, free trade, and deregulation; but for her, the technical arguments and insights were in harmony with her fundamental instincts. Incidentally, these were the same free trade principles, openness, and economic liberalism of Hayek—and later Friedman—that Winston Churchill, 50 years earlier, felt that the conservative party had abandoned. Amongst the key decisive arguments was the realisation that printing money in excess would eventually affect prices, economic stability, and the government. In order to stop inflation, they had to restrict the quantity of money; otherwise, too much money would be chasing too few goods. With her Chancellors Geoffrey Howe, Nigel Lawson, and John Major, she was able to pursue monetarism policies (Thatcher: 1995).

Although, in principle, monetarism is very independent of fiscal policy, linking the two together in a financial strategy appeared to make sense since it provided a basis for monetary restriction and declining inflation to go hand in hand with falling nominal and real interest rates, thus providing a stimulus to private sector demand. Perhaps equally important was the feeling that monetary policy and monetary targeting would, in turn, make it more likely that monetary restrictions would pull down inflation with little effect on output and employment.

The conversion to monetary policy was a combination of ideology, intellectual conviction, and the rather disastrous macro-economic experience of the 1970s. This shift to monetarism as the new way forward was enshrined in the adoption of the Medium-Term Financial Strategy (MTFS) in the budget of 1980 where the Thatcher government launched a four-year plan that incorporated both fiscal and monetary policy to reduce the rate of inflation, reduce budgetary deficits, and generate economic growth over an initial period of four years. A month before, the MTFS was supplemented by sterling's membership in the Exchange Rate Mechanism.

The 1980 budget was conspicuous not only because it introduced a severe fiscal squeeze at a time of recession but also because it reverted to the much earlier practice of controlling public expenditure through cash limits. With the acceleration of inflation through the late 1960s and 1970s, governments of all complexions turned to the practice of planning government expenditure and prices in real terms. In effect, government departments asked for and were guaranteed quantities of resources, equipment, and personnel, irrespective of the price that would have to be paid. Actual money expenditure was therefore open-ended and dependable on the prices at the time. Thus, government spending departments were protected from general inflation and particular inflation on purchased goods and services. Although there was some logic to the method, it did mean that the Treasury had no idea what government expenditure would be in money terms and would have to be financed out of taxation or borrowing until after the event. There was also no pressure on spending departments to make more efficient use of resources, even if the price of items rose. The return to cash limits meant not that real resource planning was abolished, but that once the real resource allocation had been agreed for a coming year and the cash expenditure calculated at current prices, only a general expected inflation factor could be applied to the totals to fix the cash limit for the spending periods.

Although attacked as irrational by many economists, the practice could and still can be defended on two grounds. Firstly, it acted as an automatic inflation stabiliser, and secondly, it gave ministers, public sector officials, and trades unions an incentive to support anti-inflationary policies. From this point of view, the 1981 budget was crucial because it established without doubt the government's determination to pursue anti-inflationary policies.

The priority in the first budget was to cut income tax. The 1981 budget saw the conservative government of Mrs Thatcher increase personal taxes in order to control the deficit and beat inflation. The economic strategy had four elements: first, the fight against the deep-rooted inflation which had become engrained in the British system. The second priority was to bring. public sector finances under control. The third element was to promote private enterprise and ownership, shifting the balance away from the state to private companies. Finally, there was the programme of structural reforms to make markets work more efficiently; also known as the supply-side revolution. The supply-side revolution included trade union reform, abolishing exchange controls, and controls on prices, incomes, and dividends. They promoted competition in financial services, reduced controls over private rented housing, and gave public sector tenants the right to buy their own homes at large discounts. All the changes were made in the public sector, in education, the NHS, and local government (Thatcher: 1995, 573-576).

It was hardly surprising that a strategy associated with a 2½ fold increase in unemployment came under such stiff criticism and political hostility. The real impact of the Thatcher government's new thinking was most clearly felt in the privatisation programme of state-owned and state-provided services. The programme covered both denationalisation and liberalisation (the relaxation or abolition of the state's monopoly of service delivery). Mrs Thatcher believed that publicly owned industries were inefficient and an obstacle to the creation of a more adaptive and spontaneous economy, and since the nationalised industries were only supported amongst the Labour Party and the public sector trades unions, there was no problem getting rid of them (Kavanagh: 1990: 250).

A squeeze on social expenditure was accompanied by various measures to encourage the private provision of services, such as hospital beds, places in schools, and private insurance schemes. These have been quite separate from the moves to expand the contracting out to the private sector of work such as catering and building maintenance in the services that have continued to be provided by the state. The two have tended to be confused under the catch-all label of privatisation, but they are very distinct.

In July 1982, in a lecture given by Geoffrey Howe, he said that for the sake of economic reasons, there were powerful reasons why the government should be ready to consider how far private provision and individual choice could supplement or replace the role of government in some cases in health, social security, and education (Howe: 1982, 21). The way forward involved a review of their commitments to a consideration of market mechanisms as a means of promoting greater cost consciousness and of extending choice (Howe: 1982, 22).

During her first term, from 1979-84, Margaret Thatcher focused on her brand of monetarism, which was characterised by the privatisation of state assets which had been nationalised by the Atlee government of 1945-51. Industries like steel, railways, the airways, airports, aerospace, and utilities like gas, electricity, telecoms and water. The British public were turned into shareholders as shares were sold, at times below the market value. While this created wealth for many, it also arguably increased the gap between those who had, and those who didn't have; thereby, increasing inequality.

The second economic strand of Thatcherism was deregulation. There was increased competition in markets, tight controls on the printing of money, and deregulation in the financial industry. Deregulation meant that new firms entered previously closed markets like telecoms and energy: competition increased, prices fell, enabled by new technologies. Competition promoted the sale of public housing to tenants and reduced government expenditure on healthcare, education, and housing. This involved opening up council services to the market, allowing private firms to competitively bid to run public services more efficiently, at lower cost, using new technologies and methods than the public sector. This was seen as a potential win for the government in terms of being able to distance itself from operational delivery, and a win for citizens through improved service delivery, than the inefficient public services that they had become accustomed to. Critics argued private firms would cut costs to offer inferior services and make a profit at the expense of taxpayers. The years since, has shown that is criticism and fear was justified. The third strand of her approach was in relation to trades unions, where she applied the Hayekian playbook of imposing legal restrictions on unions, reducing their powers and ultimately triumphing over the coal miners in their strikes of 1984 to 85.

Immediately after the 1939–1945 war, the UK economy experienced strong growth with moderate inflation. However, in the 1970s, inflation rose to double figures, reaching 25 percent (Office for National Statistics: 2022). In part, this inflation was caused by rising oil prices, which tripled in the 1970s, and rising wages, in part due to trades unions demanding higher wages to keep up with the rising cost of living (Pettinger: 2022). The effect of the upsurge of inflation is that the inflationary costs were on top of the expected public spending, which was made worse because government and Treasury assumptions were that spending commitments could and would be financed out of economic growth: a growth that was never achieved. Between 1973 and 1975, public spending was out of control, rising from 51 percent of GDP to 59 percent. Between 1953 and 1973, spending on social welfare programmes, which included education, social security, and health, grew from 32 percent to 44 percent. In contrast, spending on defence, law and order, and foreign affairs fell from 45 percent to 27 percent (Rose: 1985). In 1976, cash limits were imposed on government departments, and departmental allocations from then on included a figure for future inflation, but there was no commitment that the government would increase spending to match the inflation figure or, indeed, the inflation reality. i.e., the combined Budget and Public Expenditure White Paper in March 1982 reaffirmed the Medium-Term Financial Strategy's (MTFS) plan to cut some taxes, and for the first time, public expenditure was planned in cash terms. Geoffrey Howe's 1979 budget cut the basic rate of income tax from 33 percent to 30 percent, which was reduced from 33 percent to 25 percent in 1988 and cut the top rate of income tax from 83 percent to 60 percent, reducing it to 40 percent by 1988. The Thatcher administration further cut the tax on investment income from 98 percent to 75 percent (Thatcher: 1995). These actions began the shift from direct to indirect taxes.

The conservative government abolished the higher rate of VAT, establishing a new unified standard rate of 15 percent, which meant that Budget 1979, increased the rate of VAT from 8 percent to 15 percent Geoffrey Howe said he expected that this would increase inflation by 3.5 percentage points, but he was also reducing income taxes to compensate, ensuring that VAT became a more important source of government tax revenue (Hansard: 1979). Most controversially was the introduction of the community charge, called the poll tax, which was a new local government tax charging a single rate to everyone, regardless of income.

Since the mid-1970, both labour and conservative governments have attempted – with some success—to restrain public spending. Between 1975/6 and 1977/8 the labour government managed to reduce housing and education spending by 12.4 percent and 4 percent, respectively (Public Expenditure White Paper Cmnd 7841.1980). During this time, social security spending saw an increase of 8.3 percent, and the national health service saw an increase of 2.0 percent. By 1979/80-1980/81, under a conservative government, planned spending was extremely low, with increases in social security of 2.4 percent falling to 0.7 percent by 1982/3. Spending on the National Health Service increased by 2.7 percent in 1979-81, while education spending fell by 4 percent under labour, and by 4.5 percent in 1979-81 under the conservative government. Housing saw the most dramatic changes, from -12.4 percent under a Labour government to –30.9 percent planned spending between 1980-83 under the Thatcher government.

Across the years 1975-1983, total public expenditure had reduced. The highest percentage reduction of -6.5 percent came under a labour government. The direction of lower public sector spending was slightly reversed but continued with less severity by the incoming 1979 conservative government. Total public sector spending (unadjusted for by the switch to child benefit) in 1977-79, was up by 6 percent; 4.1 percent between 1978/9-80; falling to –0.7 percent 1979-81 and 3.8 percent 1980-83 (Public Expenditure White Paper Cmnd 7841. 1980). The commitment to reducing public spending and borrowing, specifically across housing, education, and social security provided a road map of where the Thatcher government was going, and its wish to encourage incentives to work and investment. The government's ultimate goal was to use market forces and appropriate legislation to reduce real wages by reducing housing subsidies and benefits. Mrs Thatcher was seeking to use the government's social policy, supported by legislation and reduced spending, to encourage self-reliance and individualism and to move away from collectivism and the post-War consensus, which Hayek also railed against.

The manufacturing sector was hard hit during the 1982 recession, and consequently, unemployment rose to 3 million. By 1985 unemployment was still at 2.5 million. In the 1988 budget, Nigel Lawson cut the basic tax rate from 29 percent to 25 percent and higher rates to 40 percent and he also cut interest rates. These tax cuts, along with good performance from North Sea Oil, put more money in people's pockets, increasing consumer spending, which allowed an economic boom. As a result, consumer spending went up, house prices rose, which meant people felt wealthier, and it led to economic growth of over 5 percent a year. This was a classic boom-bust cycle, as it caused a rise in inflation of over 10 percent. Inflation needed to be brought under control. Mrs Thatcher did not want to join the ERM but was persuaded by her Chancellor Nigel Lawson, and the government joined the Exchange Rate Mechanism in 1990 (until 1992) which it hoped would bring inflation under control. A recession ensued in 1991 caused primarily by high interest rates, falling house prices, and an overvalued exchange rate, which paradoxically was one of the reasons why interest rates were higher than the government wanted them to be because the Chancellor wanted to follow an unofficial exchange rate of 3DM to £1.

When viewed in the context of the post-war consensus or approach, Buiter and Miller (1983) argued that the Thatcher government's return to sound money, marked an important turning point in UK macroeconomic policy-making. Buiter and Miller maintained that the 1944 white paper was seen as a commitment by the government to use policy instruments to pursue high employment, low inflation, and economic growth through Keynesian demand management. However, the desired results were not achieved, and inflation went up to 15 percent in the 1960s and 1970s. On taking office, the Thatcher government responded by spearheading a shift in emphasis, which saw them abandoning the commitment to full employment; moving away from attempts to influence prices and wages through the incomes policies that Edward Heath had adopted, and instead utilising indirect taxes. Additionally, her government used intermediate financial targets by applying MTFS, which was a counter-inflationary measure. Cumulatively, these actions marked an admission that previous governments had overreached beyond what they could control and needed to retrench. Mrs Thatcher applied supply-side economic theory and sought to keep taxes low, reducing income tax, especially on high incomes.

In the wake of Edward Heath and James Callahan being unable to manage the call for increased wages at a time of high employment, the Thatcher government was reorganising the relationship between government, the private sector, and labour. The government had decided to primarily concern itself with managing inflation, which was evidenced by the introduction of a Medium-Term Financial Strategy (MTFS). Buiter and Miller noted that after 4 years of the Thatcher government, the depression of the 1980s would be worse in real terms than the great depression, where GDP growth in the years after the depression averaged 4.7 percent and unemployment had declined from a peak of 15.6 percent in 1932 to 7.8 percent in 1937. While the UK was not on its own, it had a more exaggerated response compared to other OECD countries to the increased oil prices from 1973 to 1978, which saw the UK's inflation rate and unemployment soar.

The second term of the Thatcher government was focused on reducing public sector borrowing requirements (PSBR). Public expenditure failed to fall by 1 percent between 1979 and 1983, as earmarked in the Thatcher government's White Paper (Cmnd 7841), but instead rose at a rate of 1.5 percentage points each year, rising from 41 percent to 44 percent in 1982- 83. The areas where there was overspending were Social Security, energy trade and employment, and the rise in lending to nationalised industries. This meant that the recession had the indirect effect of increasing public spending on unemployment benefits and supporting nationalised industries to stay afloat. This, for some, was evidence of the automatic stabilisers of Keynesianism at work. For Thatcherites, however, it was the government overreaching over spending that was among the reasons why inflation needed to be controlled. In order to keep PSBR under 2 percent and reduce the burden on government expenditure, the Thatcher government set about a programme of selling the government's share in public industries, along with reducing welfare spending and the state's involvement in welfare provision.

Unemployment rose in 1979 to figures last seen in the 1930s. In 1977-1978, unemployment hovered around 5 to 6 percent. Using a new measurement of unemployment that was no longer based on those registering as unemployed but on those claiming benefits; in 1979, 1.2 million people were unemployed. In 1981, this rose to 2.8 million, and it rose to 3 million in 1983. At the same time, inflation fell from 13.4 percent in 1979 to 4.6 percent in 1983. Long-term unemployment was the most worrying part of this unprecedented increase (Government Expenditure Plans: 1983) (Employment Gazette: 1983). There was uncertainty as to whether pursuing monetarism and deflation was worth it if unemployment was going to be so high.

Looking back at the literature, the significance of Margaret Thatcher's ideological stance would lie primarily in the extent to which she succeeded in completing the breakup of the amalgam of ideas that composed the post-war social and democratic consensus, like the Fabian faith in the state; the Keynesian commitment to full employment, and the Liberal emphasis on social welfare and social security. Secondly, through what she purported economically, socially and politically; Margaret Thatcher was able to link pro-market economics, minimal state intervention and individual autonomy to core conservative beliefs around law and order; God; faith; country; pre-eminence of the family; be praised, individual responsibility; hard work; wealth and achievement. This was in antithesis to the collectivism, anti-wealth, welfare dependency and paternalism that the New Right saw as hallmarks of the left. Thatcherism in this guise had an intense popular appeal to the British public. It offered hope while finely balancing authoritarianism and populism. Excluding the populist elements, her vision was broadly and tentatively aligned with Hayek's view of a free society

The consolidation of Thatcherism and her new ideas was not only helped by the fact that the post-War consensus had already been attacked and seriously undermined, but the Labour Party was in no position to deliver material rewards. The credibility of the Fabian drive for full employment and the welfare state had been seriously impaired (Leys: 1989,103). The state encountered by the electorate played too many roles as parents, planners, teachers, and employees and had become too restrictive, bureaucratic, and paternalistic. More profoundly, the working class had undergone some significant changes: the traditional style of proletariat/working class of the 1930s and 1940s, for which the welfare state had been created, had changed, and there was now an unclear dividing line or distinction between members of the working-class who were now middle class and those who were transitioning, partly because, even though it was largely unequally distributed, the boom between 1950 and 1970 created wealth, which increased the growth in private home ownership. By the age of 30, over 60 percent of those born in the 1950s and 1960s were homeowners; this reduced to 55 percent of those born in the 1970s, and dramatically fell to only 36 percent homeownership amongst those born in the 1980s. For example, typical income for those born in the 1940s and 1950s approximately doubled, in real terms, between their late 20s and early 50s (Brewer and Wernham: 2022). For example, typical income for those born in the 1940s and 1950s approximately doubled, in real terms, between their late 20s and early 50s. Those born in the 1960s saw a rise of around a half from age 25 to 50; those born in the 1970s saw a rise of less than a quarter over 25 years (Brewer and Wernham: 2022). The increase in wealth made it possible to argue that people didn't need such an interventionist state, and after the 1970s, the post-war consensus began to give way to free enterprise as the challenge rose from the new political right of the conservative party.

The growth and dominance of free enterprise and competitive individualism were heavily influenced by those who wished to see individual liberty and self-determination increase, allowing the financial markets to be pitted against the prowess and wit of individuals to succeed or fail without an overbearing state. Whilst for many on the political left, this was about greed; those on the political right, initially leveraged their approach by deploying pragmatic, and at times religious arguments around liberty and freedom; however, with the seminal works of Friedrich von Hayek in *'The Road to Serfdom'*, 1944 and Milton Friedman in *Capitalism and Freedom* 1962, those on the right found the much need well-crafted, theoretical and academic undergirding to justify and cogently argue that their economic approach was not about greed, but about growth, protecting individuals from a controlling and overbearing state, fighting the fight against socialism and communism, which in-turn would foster economic growth in the United States of America and in Great Britain.

Hayek in *'The Road to Serfdom'*, 1944 argued that state power was a menace to individual liberty and that the real threat to freedom was the concentration of power in political hands. The involvement of the state should be curtailed because it inhibits the potential of individuals to maximise their potential. Living in and observing the United States of America, Milton Friedman argued that the negative of government was that its intervention often had the opposite effect than was initially desired. For him, therefore, only the free market enabled the true transaction of ideas, money, and resources, and nearly all forms of government intervention – except in the supply of money—were unwelcome (Friedman: 1993). Inflation occurs when the quantity of money rises more rapidly than the overall economic output in particular sectors, products, or the economy as a whole (Friedman: 1990, 254). Milton Friedman presented a challenge to the dominant economic doctrine of Keynesianism, arguing that there was a causal link between money supply and inflation, and even at the expense or risk of unemployment, it was right that the approach of monetarism had an emphasis on controlling money supply and reducing inflation. The more rapid the rise in the quantity of money in circulation, the greater the rate of inflation. Or, to put it another way; inflation becomes evident when there is a decrease in the purchasing power of cash money: this diminution is felt in real terms by the prices of goods and services in an economy increasing. If the government borrowed or printed more money, businessmen would merely push up prices, generating demand for more wages from the workforce, resulting in inflation. In order to head off this potential, Friedman advised that the money supply should not expand at a rate beyond production and that high interest rates should be used to restrict borrowing. For Friedman, if governments clearly stated this as their approach and refused to deviate from it; trades unions would realise that wage demands would need to be matched by production; otherwise, it would result in the bankruptcy of companies and increased unemployment. This in itself will keep wage demands and inflation down. In his seminal work published in 1957, *Theory of the Consumption Function*, Friedman argued that there was a distinction between how individual households viewed income and that income had two important components: permanent and transitory income, which he expressed as $Y = Yp + Yt$. Transitory or expected income affected how households spent; and in the context of increased wage demands, this could result in high inflation as households tended to spend based on anticipated and transitory income, irrespective of whether there has been increased economic output to match the demand created by wage demands or *not*.

The key debate that emerged was between the Hayekian call for competition and individual freedom and the Friedman monetarist focus on the control of money in the economy as being crucial to growth versus the Keynesian view, which sees the intervention of government, including government expenditure, as being necessary to prevent a troubled economy from getting into greater difficulty.

In the 1970s, inflation had reached 25 percent; unemployment was steadily rising, but in 1979, when Mrs Thatcher was elected Prime Minister, unemployment accelerated. The UK was experiencing double-digit inflation, which peaked at 18 percent in 1980. By the end of 1980, interest rates in the UK were 14 percent, and they dropped to 10 percent by 1982. The lowest rate of interest during the 1980s was 7.38 percent in 1988. Mrs Thatcher introduced economic policies that were aimed at reducing inflation by adopting monetarist policies, which ostensibly meant controlling the supply of money. The primary tools used were cuts in public expenditure, raising interest rates, and increasing value-added taxes (VAT) which ironically increased inflation briefly from 9 percent in May 1979 to 21.9 percent in May 1980. This saw one of the largest shifts in taxation from the rich to the poor. Mrs Thatcher was successful in reducing inflation; however, maintaining the base rate at 17 percent for 12 months from 1979 meant that manufacturing costs were too high, the exchange rate of the pound sterling was too strong, resulting in British exports slowing down, which led to a 14 percent fall in manufacturing output, and increased factory closures, resulting in unemployment rising to 3 million. High interest rates meant that manufacturing costs and unemployment remained high throughout the 1980s, partly because the UK's manufacturing sector was decimated by higher interest rates on loans, higher taxes, the offshoring of manufacturing capacity, UK output declining, and government spending cuts, which meant households had less disposable income.

The reduction in inflation, the stabilisation of public finances, and the resurgence in productivity are the most conspicuous economic successes of the Thatcher years. The most obvious failure has been the level of unemployment, and while critics blamed this on the government's contractionary fiscal and monetary policies, the government in turn blamed it on the decisions of private sector businesses (Bean and Symons: 1989, 10).

Trades unions were powerful, and there were signs that British industry was becoming increasingly uncompetitive (Pettinger: 2017. The government had previously tried to close a number of coal mines, and in 1984, the Coal Board announced that 20 uneconomic pits would have to close, putting 20,000 miners out of work (BBC: 2013). In protest at the plans, miners at the Cortonwood colliery in Yorkshire went on strike on March 5, 1984 and within a week, more than half of the country's miners were on strike, which lasted a year; after which the mine closures continued. Thatcherites were known as the *Dries*, and they represented the modern right wing of the Conservative Party, in contrast to the party's old-style moderates known as the *Wets*. Heavily influenced by the Monetarism of Milton Friedman, the Thatcherite *Dries* wanted an end to what she, and they saw as excessive government interference in the economy by moving aggressively to free markets, reducing state intervention, reducing the power of trades unions, and tackling inflation. The cumulative effect was that her tough budgetary measures meant that growth suffered, and her first term ushered in a recession, followed, in the latter part of the 1980s by a boom.

Like Hayek, Friedman's belief was that the scope of government should be limited. The differentiation between them both was that Hayek's position was based on a fear of the fascism and Nazism that occurred in Germany and Italy taking root in Britain, and so economic liberty, and the removal of coercion were key corner stones, while Friedman was purely about monetarism and the free market. Friedman saw a reduced state as a prerequisite for free market monetarism, while Hayek saw liberty and the absence of coercion as the prerequisite. Government was a problem for Friedman due to the influence of special interests, which meant that government actions often provided substantial benefits to a few, whilst imposing small costs on many (Friedman 1993: 4). For Friedman, the government's primary function was to protect the citizen from foreign enemies and to ensure law and order within its boundaries. There should be a presumption against government intervention. There were, however, two instances, on a discretionary basis, where the government was expected to intervene. Firstly, where individuals en masse were struggling, the government should intervene to provide public service. Secondly, government intervention was also necessary to enforce laws that opened up markets where closed market practises such as monopolies were operating. Friedman argued that in these types of situations, government intervention was unavoidable, but even here, it should only be pursued as long as the advantages of intervention outweighed the disadvantages.

Both Friedman and Hayek were concerned to preserve, enhance, foster, or create individual liberty, but whereas Friedman focused on substantively critiquing government intervention, Hayek's argument was a procedural one as he sought not to prohibit intervention but to contain market interventions around the principles of the rule of law which would ensure the neutral and abstract reasoning and application of laws under a constitutional system with clear and unambiguous separation of powers between the legislature, the executive, and the judiciary. It is in this regard that Thatcherism and subsequent Conservative leaders and those on the Conservative right leaned close to Hayek, for they all agree on limiting the role and involvement of government and letting the market work freely. But what Hayek did was lay out his Weberian like *Ideal Type* in, "*A Constitution of Liberty*" where he set out the parameters and the procedural and lawful way in which this should occur. While this formed the skeleton of the model for Thatcher, political pragmatism saw her and her government roll out a monetarist approach in a structured and systematic way.

Hayek was concerned about the application of arbitrary laws and execution discretion. He saw arbitrary laws and execution discretion as examples of undesirable coercive powers of the stage, which he argued should only ever be applied if confined or regulated by neutral, abstract, or generally applicable laws. His essential argument was that coercion, which is undesirable, becomes evident when the rule of law gives way to the rule of men.

What we do know is that while Friedman wanted to constrain the actions and intervention of the state, Hayek preferred that if intervention and greater state involvement were required, they would form part of the generally applicable laws, processes, and procedures and not be subject to discretion. What we have seen is that crises or periods of national upheaval result in increased government interventions. Friedman, in contrast, saw the issue as being about self-interest.

Hayek's philosophy held that immutability, the primacy of personal freedom, and the absence of coercion were the prerequisites of a free society. Along with Milton Friedman, Hayek argued that by answering their own selfish interests, individuals will contribute to the betterment and the good of all. Self-interest for Friedman did not exist only in the private sector but was evident in the public sector too. The difference for Friedman was in results, and he goes on to explain that there is one thing that you can trust everybody to do, and that is to put their interests above yours. Most new enterprises fail, so those running enterprises have strong incentives to ensure that they don't fail, or have to dip into their own pockets and as such, they have a different bottom line than those same individuals starting the same enterprise in the government, where if it fails, it can be argued that the scope of the enterprise was too small; the personal funds of those running the government enterprise are not at risk; and crucially, the government is able to increase tax on the population to stave off failure. Friedman concludes therefore that: if a private enterprise is a failure, it closes down—unless it can get a government subsidy to keep it going; if a government enterprise fails, it is expanded. In essence, the self-interest of those running either a private or state enterprise is the same (Friedman:1993, 5).

Hayek saw the self-interest of individuals as being susceptible to an invisible hand that would regulate economic activity in a beneficial manner as long as supplies were allowed to meet demands for goods at a price the public was prepared to pay. Competition would ensure that profits were not too high and that suppliers would seek cheaper and more efficient means of investment. Efficient individuals would be successful and able to maximise their benefits, which in the long run would benefit all, giving the consumer a variety of goods to choose from. Hayek's ideas were based on his craving for a free society, which rests on the premise of inherent inequality existing between members of society and their various abilities to maximise their potential within a free society.

For Hayek and Mrs Thatcher, inequality was not an anathema, as it was more beneficial than disadvantageous because it could inject dynamism and buoyancy into the economy, raising minimum and maximum earnings. Government interventions like the provision of regional aid to help the survival of manufacturing and other industries outside of London, along with actions designed to alleviate inequality and hardship, were cut back after 1979. The cuts and the rolling back of state support further exacerbated the division of wealth between the north and south of England and began to entrench the north-south divide. Those with higher incomes benefited from a steady reduction in income tax, which further increased the gap between rich and poor. Government policy had a complex impact on society's cleavages as it polarised and classified citizens as either productive, unproductive, rich, poor, northern, southern, employed, or unemployed (Jessop: 1988).

This retrenchment of government was central to the ideology of the new - political -right and its policy agenda, which saw state interference as distorting the market. The *New Right* needed people with political weight to articulate and give force to this new ideology. The momentum and credibility came from the Mont Pelerin Society, formed by Friedrich Von Hayek, Milton Friedman, and George Stigler in 1947 at a conference with thirty-nine economists, philosophers, and historians in a hotel in the Swiss village of Mont Pèlerin. Among its members was Sir Geoffrey Howe, who was Chancellor of the Exchequer from May 1979 – June 1983 and was Margaret Thatcher's longest-serving Cabinet minister. The aims and objectives of the Mont Pelerin Society (MPS) were to promote classical liberalism, preserve freedom, be anti-collectivist, and protect individuals from the extension of the arbitrary power of the state. For the MPS, there needed to be an understanding of the role of the state in order to distinguish between totalitarianism and liberalism. To that end; the MPS strongly advocated private property and competitive markets. The MPS provided the impetus for the establishment in 1957 of the Institute of Economic Affairs (IEA), which, together with the Centre for Policy Studies (CPS) (co-founded in 1974 by Alfred Sherman, Sir Keith Joseph and Margaret Thatcher), and the Adam Smith Institute (established in 1977 and chaired by Hayek to develop free market policies), gradually persuaded academics and politicians of the benefits of free enterprise over Keynesian state intervention. Hayek, initially and inadvertently, via the MPS; the IEA; the CPS; the Salisbury

Group; Geoffrey Howe; Milton Friedman, and Sir Keith Joseph were the prime influencers on Mrs Thatcher

Enoch Powell's influence on Margaret Thatcher has been downplayed because of the myopic focus of politicians, the media and many political scientists on his river of Tiber speech. From the 1960s, however, his contribution to the *New Right* was invaluable and, to some degree, incalculable as he was an early sceptic of the European Common Market. Of equal importance but much more palatable and with longevity was Sir Keith Joseph. Sir Keith Joseph's influence on Margaret Thatcher was solidified because he had been part of the 1970-1974 conservative government, and he had left that government having served in the Department of Health and Social Services, clear in his mind - due to experience and having read Friedman and Hayek - that big government spending was not the answer to curbing inflation.

In a Speech in Preston on September 5, 1974, Joseph explained that inflation was caused by governments. This speech marked a departure from conservative government policy, and some saw it as Sir Keith making a bid for the leadership of the conservative party. Joseph subscribed to Friedman's fear of inflation as a threat that could destroy our society. In a nod to Hayek's 1944, *The Road to Serfdom,* and his fear of the loss of freedom and the coercive power of a strong state, Keith Joseph said that there was a risk that well-intentioned, ineffective political parties would respond to the frustrations of the population; inadvertently or intentionally, by paving the way for those offering solutions at the cost of freedoms. Sir Keith noted that there were warnings back in the 1950s that the pernicious nature of inflation was going to adversely affect the country, and he put his hands up and accepted responsibility for the part he played in it. In this speech, Joseph noted that Maynard Keynes also believed that excessive money creation was inflationary. (Joseph: 1974). This, according to J M Keynes, isn't completely true. in *The General Theory of Employment, Interests and Money*, Keynes said that *'... the long-run relationship between the national income and the quantity of money would depend on liquidity preferences and the long-term stability or instability of prices would depend on the strength of the upward trend of the weight unit. With the rate of increase in the efficiency of the productive system'* (Keynes: 2009, 260-267). Essentially, he was arguing that it was not a fait accompli that an increase in money in the economy would cause inflation, but that it was dependent on wage increases matching the efficiency of the system of production (Keynes: 2009, 267). Joseph argued about the folly of income's policy and that incomes policies would be unable to mitigate the effects of inflation if money was pumped into the economy at a faster rate than the growth of goods and services; an awareness of supply and demand was crucial and Joseph argued that there had been a misunderstanding of Keynes and that Keynes did not in fact argue that the way to deal with medium- and long-term involuntary unemployment was to increase the money supply or to increase demand (Joseph: 1974). Keynes had argued for a better distribution between demand and supply, but sadly for Joseph; when faced with rising unemployment, successive governments simply increased public sector spending. For Joseph, this was a misunderstanding of Keynes, and on coming to office, Margaret Thatcher adopted the stance that Joseph outlined and sought to aggressively reduce public spending, which, contrary to the expectations of Sir Keith Joseph and Margaret Thatcher, caused inflation and unemployment to climb exponentially.

With the demise and rejection of Keynesian economics, post-Keynesians and Sir Keith Joseph found a common cause and seemed to agree that the economics that had been implemented in Keynes's name between 1945 and 1975 was not in fact the economics that Keynes himself had proposed. Post-Keynesians, like Skidelsky (1983), Carabelli (1988), Fitzgibbons (1988), O'Donnell (1989); Lawson and Pesaran (1985), Bateman (1987), Davis (1994), and Runde (1994) - wrote numerous books and articles about Keynes's life and his economics in order to resurrect Keynesianism and to amplify that the Keynesianism implemented was what Keynes himself would have recognised or supported (Gillies: 2003).

Margaret Thatcher had seized her opportunity when she became leader of the conservative party and later Prime Minister to disassociate herself from the policies of full employment. She, like Sir Keith Joseph, believed that socialism's push for equality, state intervention, and nationalisation had overburdened the economy and taken away individual autonomy. This then pointed her in the direction of running full pelt towards monetarism and, later, the free market economics of Hayek. Where Edward Heath panicked, she knuckled under and watched as her policies pushed unemployment spectacularly above 3 million. One of the challenges that Mrs Thatcher experienced was that her ministers and many in the Conservative Party felt it was necessary to maintain the welfare state, full employment, and high levels of public expenditure. Since the 1930, governments and former prime ministers felt that there was an electoral advantage in keeping this in place. However, Mrs Thatcher believed in individualism, thrift, and self-reliance, and according to Dennis Kavanagh, she did not have some of the bourgeois guilt that her predecessors had for the mass unemployment in the 1930s (Kavanagh: 1990, 118). It made it easier for her to act quickly and decisively. Irrespective of how cruel it may seem, for Hayek, poverty and inequality are necessary in a free society because the role of the state and of society cannot and should not be to guarantee each individual a new resource. For Hayek, the majority would ultimately benefit as long as the government's role was to enable an environment for the stimulation of individual development. Hayek did not believe that taking from the rich and giving to the poorest would achieve long-term equality: at the most, equality would be temporary, but such a move would inevitably slow down the progress of society and, more significantly, hold back those in whose name equality was being sought.

Armed with this knowledge and as an adherent of monetarism and the free market, Mrs Thatcher began to push the balance of the economy away from central state-controlled ownership and management towards the private ownership of state-owned services and utilities in gas, steel, and electricity. In addition to enabling freedom and competition, home ownership grew as a result of her government's policies, which encouraged tenants to purchase their council homes. This brought many to the realisation that there was a viable possibility of building wealth and having social mobility through property ownership. In terms of welfare provision, the conservative party and organisations like the Institute of Public Affairs were arguing for a more selective provision of welfare benefits and for the extension of the competitive market into the welfare system as preferable to the existing system of universal welfare provision. Although, not through lack of trying, the welfare state has remained largely intact, and the ideas of a mixed economy of provision in the delivery of welfare were abandoned.

The monetarist ideas of Milton Friedman were seen as an effective solution for the economic problems that were being experienced in the aftermath of the post-war consensus and the implementation of Keynesian economic policies. Friedman held that excessive government spending pushed too much money into the economy, resulting in inflation that devalued people's income and reduced their overall quality of life.

Monetarism became discredited in Britain when it was seen that inflation had fallen. In its place came a renewed commitment to the free market economy, in which strict budgetary controls would be used to limit public spending. Local authorities would be rate-capped, and there would be a general reduction in taxation. The action of the government would enable the restoration of the free market. Trade union power would be curbed, bureaucracy reduced, and nationalised industries would be returned to the private sector.

Hayek believed in personal liberty, which rested on the recognition of our inevitable ignorance in relation to all factors of life. He saw liberty as important and essential for a progressive society because it left room for the unforeseeable and unpredictable, with the understanding that we, as individuals, groups, and institutions, are so limited that we need to rely on the independent and competitive efforts of many. Important to Hayek's work was his argument for an elite-style society where knowledge, once achieved, would be made available for the benefit of all.

Hayek saw the role of businessmen and entrepreneurs as immensely important in this free society. He wanted them to have free reign in leading society forward. This coincided with the Thatcherite policies of private enterprise and rolling back the state so that economic growth could develop freely.

Money Supply and a Free Society

In his address to the Geneva Gold and Monetary Conference at Lausanne, Switzerland, on September 25, 1975, Professor Hayek made it known that he saw the chief root of the then-monetary problem as the sanction of scientific authority given to Keynes and the Keynesian idea that by increasing the aggregate of money expenditure, one could ensure prosperity and full employment. Hayek noted that historically, inflation had always been a problem and that it was only during the rise of prosperous modern industrial systems and the imposition of the gold standard that, over a period of around 200 years, inflation had been controlled, resulting in prices – at the end of that period - being about where they had been at the beginning. This was undoubtedly a unique period of monetary stability in which the gold standard imposed upon monetary authorities a discipline that prevented them from abusing their powers as they had done nearly all the time previously (IEA: 1976, 46).

Hayek excoriated the rehabilitated theories of Keynes and argued that what Keynes had advocated to alleviate unemployment would in fact make it worse in the long run. What Keynes had done, according to Hayek was, through a succession of new theories, attempt to justify a belief that would not withstand the rigorous analysis of the price mechanism (Garrison & Barry, 2014, 111).

Hayek was not averse to full employment; but for him; the issue was about how it could be achieved. There was no doubt in Hayek's mind that employment could be rapidly increased and a position of full employment achieved in the shortest possible time by means of monetary expansion. But what was questionable in Hayek's mind was that the kind of employment that would be created in this way would be inherently unstable, and that to create employment by this means would be to perpetuate high levels of fluctuations. What Hayek stressed was that to aim at the maximum levels of employment that could be achieved in the short run by means of monetary policy was essentially the policy of the desperado, who had nothing to lose and everything to gain from a short period of high employment. For Hayek, this was the manufacture of employment. It is quite a complex process and operates by causing temperature changes in the distribution of demand, drawing both unemployed and already employed workers into jobs that will disappear with the end of inflation (Hayek: 1939, 70).

At the time of this address, the theory purported by Keynes had already been discredited. However, Hayek still felt the need for concern over the fact that there was a generation of economists who knew nothing else other than Keynesianism. Hayek argued that it was the responsibility of future policymakers to protect our money against those economists whose short-term effectiveness would secure their popularity but serve no real benefit for the country. Hayek argued that even though Keynesianism as a doctrine had fallen from intellectual respectability, its threat to the chances of a sensible monetary policy was growing, and he saw it as remarkable that people had not fully realised how much irreparable damage had already been done, particularly in Britain, where it originated.

For Hayek, experience ought to have taught most people about the importance of having a stable monetary system and that the increased role of government had been responsible and as much a cause of the instability that had been experienced (Keynes: 1919, 220). With this in mind, Hayek stated that it was understandable for some to feel that it would be better if governments were deprived of their control over monetary policy. With this thought process, it was logical to want to rely on the spontaneous forces of the market to set satisfactory mediums of exchange, as in other market-led activities (Hayek: 2011. 451). Alas, for Hayek, this is now not only politically impractical, but it would be undesirable because. Firstly, if society had been allowed to develop freely and if governments had never interfered; a monetary arrangement would probably have evolved that would not have required deliberate control. For example, the use of credit instruments as money or close substitutes for money has meant that we now no longer have the choice of being able to rely on any monetary-based self-regulating mechanism as we have no knowledge of alternatives to the credit institutions that modern businesses rely on (Hayek: 1960, 451). Secondly, moreover, Hayek saw that there are circumstances that we certainly cannot hope to change by merely altering our monetary arrangements, and this makes it inevitable that this control is exercised by the government (Hayek: 1960, 452).

Hayek posited three fundamental reasons for this state of affairs. Firstly, referring to all money at all times, he explains why changes in the relative supply of money are so much more disturbing than changes in any other circumstances that could affect prices and production. Here, money is seen as a kind of loose joint in the otherwise self-steering mechanism of the market. It is a loose joint that can interfere with the adjusting mechanism and cause recurrent misdirection of production unless these effects are anticipated and deliberately counteracted. The reason this happens is because, unlike ordinary commodities, money serves not by being used up but by being handed on; hence, the consequences of a change in the supply of money or the demand for it do not directly lead to a new equilibrium (Hayek 1960: 325; 1979: 5). For example, an addition to the stock of money simply creates a new demand, which in its nature is temporary and passing. It also sets in motion further effects that will reverse the effects of the initial increase in demand (Hayek: 1960). Those who first received the money will, in turn, spend it on other things. Like the ripple in a pool, increased demand will spread itself throughout the whole economic system, temporarily altering relative prices in a way that will persist as long as the quantity of money continues to increase but will be reversed when the increase comes to an end. This is the flaw with increasing the supply of money. The second fundamental reason for this state of affairs, according to Hayek, refers to all monetary systems where the supply of money is closely related to credit, which all modern economic life rests on. And thirdly, the fundamental reasons for this state of affairs relate to the volume of government expenditure, which, in the future, one may hope to change, but currently, it is a situation that we must accept for the time being (Hayek: 1960;1979).

An important strand of thought that underlies Professor Hayek's ideas on the economy and monetary framework concerns the government's control of monetary policy, which for him was a chief cause of inflation and at all times has been the chief cause of the depreciation of the currency (Hayek: 1960, 454). Major inflations have been the result of governments diminishing the coin or issuing excessive quantities of paper money. Hayek saw the weakness of political control of money and the problematic effects of group interests because, as governments strove towards a particular aim rather than merely maintaining a self-correcting spontaneous order, they became less able to avoid serving sectional interests (Hayek: 1988, 86; 1960, 176). Sectional interests are all harmful, except when they protest against restrictions imposed upon them for the benefit of other interests. Hayek goes on to say that the politician, acting on the Keynesian maxim that in the long run we are all out of office, does not care if his successful cure of unemployment is bound to produce more unemployment in the future (Lewis: 2022, 372). The politicians who will be blamed for this situation will not be those who created it, but those who cured it. What, for Hayek, was happening was that governments were using their money and position to defraud and plunder the people. Nevertheless, the rights of governments to issue money should not be done away with, only their exclusive right to do so and their power to force people to use and accept it at a particular price (Hayek,1976:17. He believed that there should be a choice of money, and there was no reason why people should not be able to choose whether they want to buy or sell for Franks, pounds, dollars, German marks, or ounces of gold. Hayek had no objection to governments issuing money, but he believes their position is one of monopoly, and their powers to limit the kinds of money in which contracts may be concluded within their territory and to determine the rate at which monies can be exchanged are indeed very harmful. What Hayek is advocating is that all the members of the European Economic Community mutually bind together and not post any restrictions on the free use within their territories of one another's currencies (Hayek,1976:17).

For Hayek, there could be no more effective check against the abuse of money by the government than if people were left free to choose and refuse currency they distrusted or had no confidence in. This would induce the government to keep their money stable, knowing that its stability would dictate the value of their currency. Depriving governments of their powers to protect their money from competition was, for Hayek, a good thing (Lewis: 2022, 374).

Employers would see it in their advantage to offer low wages, anticipating a rise in prices, but would pay wages in a currency they trusted. This would take away the power of governments to counteract excessive wage claims because the currencies of trusted countries pursuing responsible monetary policies would displace unreliable currencies.

CHAPTER 4

The Perils of Inflation

> *'Everyone has a plan until they
> get punched in the mouth'*
> (Mike Tyson: 1997)

Hayek's fear of inflation came from his experience of inflation in his homeland, Austria, after the First World War. Hayek realised that very few people would advocate a continuous increase in prices, but erroneously, people believe that deflation is much more to be feared than inflation, and therefore, there has been a persistent error of governments moving in the direction of inflation rather than deflation. Stability can only be achieved by correcting small movements in any direction, and because we do not know how to keep prices stable, the determination to avoid deflation at any cost must result in cumulative inflation (Hayek: 1960, 330). Hayek is very doubtful that deflation is more harmful than inflation. He believed that moderate inflation was generally pleasant while it proceeded, whereas deflation was immediate and acutely painful. There is no need in Hayek's mind to take precautions against a practice whose bad effects will be immediately and strongly felt, but there is a need for precautions wherever there is action that is immediately pleasant or releases temporary difficulties, but in the long run its effects are more devastating.

Hayek believed this firstly because inflation tended to produce conditions where people were likely to make larger profits than usual and most business enterprises succeed with very few failures. In *A Tiger by the Tail 1972*, Hayek explained that during this time of high inflation, the fact that profits prove to be greater than expected and a larger number of ventures turn out to be successful, produces an atmosphere that encourages and is favourable to risk-taking. Those who would normally be driven out of business in normal times, survive. This situation will only last as long as people expect prices to continue to rise at the same rate (103). When prices begin to slump and rise no more than had been expected, profits will also fall, leaving many businesses in precarious positions closing their doors and laying off staff (ibid).

The two crucial points for Hayek are that the stimulating effect of inflation will only operate as long as it has not been foreseen. As soon as it has become apparent, for it to retain its initial stimulating effect, it will have to continue at a rate always faster than expected. If, in such a situation, prices rose less than expected, their effect would be the same as that of unforeseen deflation.

The second crucial point for Hayek is that inflation can never be more than a temporary occurrence, and even its beneficial effect can only last as long as someone is being cheated and people's expectations are disappointed. Inflation is dangerous and pernicious because the harmful effects of even small doses of inflation can only be held at bay by larger doses of inflation. Once it has continued for some time, even the prevention of further acceleration will create a situation where it will be difficult to avoid a spontaneous deflation (Hamowy: 2011, 459). Learning from our experiences, Hayek asserts that it is probable that we should be able to prevent serious depressions by preventing the inflations which regularly precede them, but there is very little that we can do to cure them once they have set in. The time that we should worry about depression is, unfortunately, when it is farthest from our minds (Hamowy: 2011, 459).

Both inflation and deflation produce their own peculiar effects by causing unexpected price changes, and they are both bound to disappoint expectations twice over. The first comes when prices prove to be higher or lower than they were expected, and the second, as more sooner happens, these price changes come to be expected and cease to have the effect that their unforeseen occurrence had. The difference between inflation and deflation is that with the former, the pleasant surprise comes first and the reaction later: while with the latter, deflation, the first effect on business is distressing Hayek: 1960, 458).

These considerations would seem to suggest that, on balance, probably some mechanical rule aimed at what is desirable in the long run and ties the hands of authorities in short-term decisions is likely to produce a better monetary policy than principles that give the authorities more power and discretion and thereby make them more susceptible to both political pressure and their own inclination to overstate the urgency of the circumstances of the moment.

The danger that inflation will continue is not so much due to the strength of those who will deliberately advocate it as to the weakness of the opposition. For Hayek, the difficulty of preventing inflation is political and not economic (Hayek, 1960;337). For Milton Friedman, inflation is a disease that is dangerous and sometimes fatal if not checked in time. Inflation is not peculiar to capitalist countries, nor is it a communist phenomenon; it is a monetary phenomenon (Friedman, 1980:298). Professor Hayek saw it as pretty certain that a drift towards more and more state control will not cease unless we stop the inflationary trend. There is no doubt in his mind that inflation produces increased dependency on government, and it is no accident that inflationary policies are generally advocated by those who want more government control. The accusation of wanting more government control is not one that is only levelled at socialist's who argue for a greater role for the state, but ironically, Margaret Thatcher, in 1979, wanted greater government control – which resulted in high inflation, in order to roll back the state. Hayek believed that any continued rise in prices is dangerous because once we begin to rely on its stimulating effect, we will be committed to a course that will leave us no choice but to choose between more inflation on the one hand and paying for our mistake through a recession or depression on the other. This cycle of depression is what followed Mrs Thatcher's economic policies of the 1980s. For Hayek, even a moderate degree of inflation was too dangerous because it tied the hands of governments. The only way Hayek saw to stop the drift towards increased government control was to concentrate efforts on monetary policy, as Mrs Thatcher did; unfortunately, this had catastrophic consequences for growth and also counterintuitively created a strong state at war with its working class.

Another effect of inflation is that it makes it increasingly difficult for people of moderate means to provide for their old age; it discourages saving and encourages debt. By destroying the middle class, it creates a dangerous gap between the completely property-less and the wealthy that is so characteristic of societies that have gone through prolonged inflation, which is the cause of so much tension in those societies. Even more ominous is the wider psychological effect and the spreading amongst the population of disregard for long-range views and exclusive concerns about immediate advantages that already dominate public policy.

For Hayek, price stability must be the primary objective of monetary policy. During the 200 years preceding 1914, when Britain had aligned to the gold standard, price levels so far as could be measured, fluctuated around a constant level, ending up pretty much where they had started and rarely changing by more than 1/3, above or below. Unrealized by Hayek is that a fluctuation from 1/3 above to one third below an average implies a fall of 50 percent of a peak, twice as high as the trough. Immediately after the war, post-war Britain's, economy was running at its maximum capacity; unemployment varied between about 1 percent and 2 percent of the whole employable population. This high level of employment had been matched by a high rate of utilisation of industrial plants and by bulging order books. The argument supporting this running of the economy at maximum capacity was that it avoided the waste and social evils of unemployment and was seen as conducive to a high rate of growth, which Britain so badly needed after the Second World War. For Hayek, this argument was an illusion.

Apart from creating a constant danger of inflation, there were many disadvantages to too high a level of economic activity. For example, there is a high likelihood of it leading to a waste of resources through bottlenecks; it encourages firms to order too much material; firms hold onto labour in excess of need; creates conditions in which the inefficient can survive; and breeds an attitude in the minds of the workers and management that is unhelpful to rapid growth. Hayek believed that a society willing to work below capacity was more likely to make better use of its opportunities for growth and outstrip in wealth than one that was constantly striving to keep all its resources in use.

On the face of it, Hayek's position seems to be an argument for mass unemployment. Hayek rejected this and sees it as an argument for balancing the advantages of a high level of unemployment against the disadvantage of overfull employment. Hayek concludes by adding that the experience of post-war Britain suggests that we have been operating above, but not always very far above, the critical range. If unemployment fluctuated between 2 percent and 3 percent instead of between 1 percent and 2 percent, with a corresponding increase in reserve capacity in capital, it could make a big difference both to the behaviour of prices and to the ultimate pace of economic growth.

In contrast, Keynes argued that the price of money should be kept cheap for as long as possible in order to deter savings; to provide affordable loans to businesses that would then employ workers; that taxation should be slashed so that people had cash to spend on the goods that created jobs; and finally; governments should employ the unemployed, and if necessary, they should borrow money as the debt would be paid back by those in work paying income and other taxes.

For Hayek, the Keynesian-style stimulus would, in the medium term, create jobs, but in the long term, the market would become distorted so that when the stimulus was removed, employers would be left making goods that were no longer needed and having employees that they could not pay.

Labour Unions and Unemployment In a Free Society

Hayek feared inflation because, to achieve the goal aimed at, it would have to constantly accelerate, and accelerating inflation would make it virtually impossible to have an effective and orderly economy, and an inflationary economy would make higher levels of unemployment much more inevitable than what it was designed to prevent.

Hayek maintained that the Keynesian diagnosis developed in the journal *Theory of Employment and Money* (1936) was fallacious and that, although there seemed to have been several decades of high or full employment, the fallacy of *Theory of Employment and Money* was being revealed because the cause of unemployment was not inadequate demand arising from inadequate total income but the disproportionate levels of wages and how they equated to the demand for labour and its supply in each sector of the economy. It had become clear that while inflation could periodically absorb unemployment, it was by no means the solution for unemployment, as it made it worse in the long run; nor was it the way to ensure full employment. Finally, inflation was a continuing and accelerating process that, for Hayek, could destroy the currency, money, institutions, and ultimately society.

Hayek's belief was that Keynes would not have approved of policies pursued after him, and now that demand management had failed, new policies had to be devised. The question for policymakers was how to provide for more flexibility in the price of labour and how to make labour markets work more effectively. In the 1930s, the argument for inflation to reduce real wages was that money wages were not flexible downward, i.e., that wage reductions were politically impossible. Hayek sees no other way to full employment but does not know how or how soon it can be achieved. Some policies, based on the assumption that flexibility is politically impossible, did not, for Hayek provided alternatives that operate in the long run or that are compatible with a free society. The only way is by revising long-established resistances to change in consumer demand. With technology and the reform of long-established laws governing collective bargaining and the labour market.

Hayek says he would not predict what chances there are of ensuring that relative wage rates are determined by market forces to balance demand and the supply of labour. He suggests how the impulse of 1975 should be handled. He would stop the increase in the supply of money, or at least reduce it to the real rate of growth in output. This would be done immediately and gradually. Also, there would have to be a restructuring of the wage system. In spite of some differences with the monetarists, Professor Hayek is arguing essentially for policy to reform the labour markets on the grounds that monetary policy alone cannot counter unemployment and alleviate inflation, and perhaps it is here that economic analysis and policy should increasingly concentrate.

For Hayek, unions were an important obstacle in this battle. Public policy concerning the unions had moved from one extreme to the other, from the time when union activities were seen as wholly illegal to the point where they; according to Hayek had become uniquely privileged institutions to which the general rules of the law did not apply. Hayek aaw them as the only important instance in which the government has obviously failed in its prime function—the prevention of coercion and violence.

The development and relative freedom attached to unions have been assisted by the fact that, at first, unions were able to appeal to the general principles of liberty and thus retain the backing of the liberals after discrimination against them had ceased and they had acquired privileged status. The mass of the population, according to Hayek, had not realised what had really happened and had not understood that they were still supporting the aspirations of unions in the belief that the struggle was still for 'freedom of association', when in fact this term had lost its meaning and the real issue was the freedom of the individual to join or not to join a union Hayek, 1972: 75,77).

This confusion, Hayek argued, was due in part to the rapidity with which the character of the problem had changed in many countries. Voluntary associations of workers had only just become legal when they began to use coercion to force unwilling workers into membership and to keep non-members out of employment. More than often, a labour dispute is not about a disagreement over pay or the conditions of employment; it is an attempt on the part of the union to force unwilling workers to join. The public was not, as yet aware that the existing legal position of unions was fundamentally wrong and that the whole basis of free societies was threatened by the powers of the unions (Hayek, 1972, 77).

Hayek states that his argument was not directed against labour unions. Neither was it to be confined to the practises that were recognised as abuse, but it was directed at some of their powers that were now widely accepted as legitimate, if not, as their sacred right. Hayek asserted that his case was further strengthened by the fact that unions had often shown restraint in exercising certain powers. It is precisely because, in the existing legal climate, they could do more than they did, and because we owe it to the moderation and good sense of many union leaders that the situation was not made worse, that we can afford to allow the present state of affairs to continue (Hayek, 1972, 77).

It is important to stress that the coercion unions have been permitted to exercise is contrary to all principles of freedom under the law and is primarily the coercion of fellow workers (ibid). Whatever true coercive power unions may be able to wield over employers is a consequence of this primary power of coercion over other workers. The right of voluntary agreement between workers and the right of workers to withhold services are in question; however, the right to strike, though a normal right, is not an inalienable right because, in certain employments, it should be written into the terms that the worker should forfeit this right. Such employment would involve long-term obligations on the part of the worker, and any attempts to break such contracts should be illegal (ibid).

The chief danger that Hayek saw in the current development of unions is that by establishing effective monopolies in the supply of different kinds of labour, the unions will prevent competition from acting as an effective regulator (Hayek, 1972, 84). In the allocation of resources. But if competition becomes ineffective as a means of such regulation, some other means will have to be adopted in its place. The only alternative to the market, however, is direction by authority. Hayek was adamant that this type of direction cannot be left in the hands of the unions or any unified organisation of labour, because it would become not simply the strongest power in the state but the power completely controlling the state. This type of socialist planning, was not what unions wanted and it was in their best interest to avoid it (Hayek, 1972, 83-84).

The ideas of Milton Friedman are worth noting here as he argued that unions were a favourite scapegoat and were accused of using their monopoly powers to force up wages, which in turn drove up costs and wages. Friedman cites Japan and Brazil, where unions were trivially important. In both counties, trades unions were under tight government control, but at the time, both countries had the same level of inflation as in the UK. What is to be remembered is that wage increases in excess of increases in productivity were a result of inflation and not the cause of it. Contrary to Hayek, Milton Friedman believed that inflation occurs when the quantity of money rises more rapidly than output, and the more rapid the rise in the quantity of money per unit of output, the greater the rate of inflation. This, in economics, was a certainty (Friedman: 1990, 254).

To summarise, Hayek sees three main reasons for the current state of economies. Firstly, the changes in the relative supply of

The Perils of Inflation

money are so much more disturbing than changes in other circumstances that could affect prices and production. Second, in most systems, the supply of money is closely related to credit, and finally, government expenditure and other circumstances we may hope to change in the future must remain as they are for the time being in order to prevent large-scale disruption of the system (Hayek:1960, 452).

Underscoring all this is the point that the government, through control of money, had diminished the coin and had issued excessive quantities of paper money, which was the chief cause of inflation. The only way to resist the drift towards further state control was by controlling and stopping inflation, because the effects of inflation created an increased dependency of the citizen on the government.

Hayek is against the idea of the economy running at maximum capacity. The reasons are that this situation leads to a waste of resources, holds onto labour in excess of need, and also creates conditions where the ineffective can survive, which is highly unconducive to growth. Trade unions also present a threat to free society because they hold employers to ransom, and Hayek believed their power to coerce fellow workers was unacceptable.

Labour Unions and Unemployment

In *The Constitution of Liberty* (1960) Hayek rails against planned, or deterministic, attempts to manage the economy. Given the levels of wealth in our societies, he argues that it is not unreasonable for citizens to expect the security of minimum levels of food, shelter, or clothing, and he accepts the need for social insurance. What he is, however, vehemently against is security of work and pay, which for him has an insidious effect on society because of the way particular trades carve out niches for themselves to the disadvantage of others. Hayek maintains that where a trade secures improved services, such as higher wages, they exclude others. Where demand has fallen, it leads to increased unemployment, which Hayek argues is because the striving for security leads to wider insecurity. Those left outside the range of sheltered occupations feel the full effect of this, and Hayek sees this as the cruel exploitation of one class over another. This has been made possible by the 'regulation of competition' rather than enabling a free market. The regulation of competition leads to the stabilisation of prices and wages while securing the income of some; it also makes the position of others precarious.

Hayek argues that where unions control the workers in a company or an industry, they can exercise unlimited pressure on employees, and they can also practically expropriate the owner and command the whole return of his enterprise (Hayek, 2011; 388). Because this will never be in the interests of all workers, this can only be achieved by coercing some workers against their interests. While Hayek is against any form of 'coercion' he somehow sees the competition in the market as being almost immune from being coercive.

For Hayek, unions engage in wage fixing, which results in keeping lower-paid workers lower-paid by preventing them from entering particular industries. The owners will agree to the wage only because they know that the union can keep others out. Where fixing will therefore keep wages higher than they would otherwise be; they also keep other wages lower than they ought to be. This is what Hayek calls money wages. This money wage exceeds the increase in real wages, and it is only possible without producing unemployment because the money wage is made ineffective by inflation. For Hayek, 'the natural aim of the union is to induce all workers to join them' (Hayek, 2001; 393). He saw the chief reasons unions were able to coerce workers was because union shop and picketing were sanctioned by legislation.

In the 18th century, under the Combination Acts of 1799 and 1800, strikes were made illegal, and although these acts were removed by 1825, it was still difficult to strike in the UK until the 1871 Trade Union Act allowed unions to incorporate into legal entities. The Trade Union Act of 1825 resulted in an increase in union formation and industrial action. However, during the First World War (1914-1918), trades union strikes reduced. However, after the war, as employers attempted to reduce wages, trades union activity increased, and at the time of the 1926 general strike, 2.8 million workers were on strike.

Inflation rose sharply in the late 1970s, and trades unions requested high wages. Which led to the 1978–1979 Winter of Discontent, which ultimately led to the election of Margaret Thatcher in May 1979.

Between 1979 and 1981, manufacturing employment fell by 17 percent, and manufacturing output fell by 20 percent. (Nickel:1985). Up until 1983, 2 million jobs in industry and 1.7 million in manufacturing were lost during Margaret Thatcher's first term. It would be unfair to lay this entirely at her door because employment in British industry began to fall in the mid-1950s and in manufacturing in the mid-1960s. What, however, was extraordinary was the rate of job loss in such a short period.

From the perspective of the Thatcherites, the unions were too strong and the reduction in manufacturing jobs and increased unemployment between 1979 and 1983 was due to workers and trades unions being unreasonable rather than the outcome of her economic policies, in part this was also due to her dislike for unions with their closed shops and like Hayek, she saw this as uniquely based on monopoly and coercion, which, as Hayek described, was supported by legislation. The Conservative government saw it as a good outcome if they were able to curtail the restrictive practises of the unions. In his June 1984 Mais lecture[1] entitled *'The British Experiment'*, Chancellor Nigel Lawson, said that *'a very significant part of the increase in unemployment… [was] simply the emergence into the open of the unsustainable disguised unemployment of the second-half of the 1970s, when overmanning -in manufacturing in particular - was rife'.*

Lawson went on to state, that what he intended to do in the medium term, was to provide freedom for the markets to work within a framework of firm monetary and fiscal discipline. Lawson explained that this approach was in contrast to the post-war trend of ad hoc government interference with free markets resulting in financial indiscipline. The approach had led to stagnation, unemployment and accelerating inflation. This for Lawson was the experiment that failed. Lawson's explanation as to why this flawed journey had been embarked upon was 'because of political and electoral pressures which in a democracy gave them no option. He went on; 'The true British experiment is a political experiment. It is the demonstration that trades union power can be curbed within a free society and that inflation can be eradicated within a democracy' (Lawson: 1984). In this speech, Lawson singlehandedly overturned the post-war economic consensus.

Employment in the industrial sectors of the UK fell so much and so fast after 1979 partly because, as Nigel Lawson said, the unions were engaged in overmanning, but also because of the increase in the exchange rate of the pound between 1979 and January 1981 when exchange rates rose by 45 percent, due to

---

[1] The Mais lecture was established in 1978 to honour Lord Mais, a former Lord Mayor of the City of London and Chancellor of the University.

the monetarist policies of the Conservative government. The pound had been strengthening under the impact of North Sea oil since 1978, but there is little doubt that it was the expectation of the tightening of money through policy that accounted for most of the upward movement from 1979 to 1981. As a policy position, the policy approaches adopted towards unions where experimental in that they weren't rigorously assessed in terms of the long-term economic effects on the country and the economy in the same way that fiscal policies were modelled. This is particularly prescient when we recap Hayek's position, as he argued in *Use of Knowledge* that no one person or organisation can know enough. Thatcherites and the *New Right* therefore diverged from Hayek, and on this issue, leaned towards monetarism and attempted to control the money supply and bear down in an overbearing, coercive and authoritarian way on trades unions. The effect was that the industrial sectors of the economy were weakened, which increased the need for imported products from across the world, which in turn rendered British industry unprofitable, resulting in mass redundancies and record high unemployment in the 1980s.

The response of the Thatcher Conservative government to trades unions was the introduction of legislation to restrict trade union power. The Employment Act 1980, restricted the definition of lawful picketing to those who were themselves parties to the dispute and who were picketing at the premises of their own employer. It also introduced ballots on the existence of closed shops, and at least 80 percent of the workers in a particular industry needed to support the strike for it to be maintained.

The 1982 Employment Act outlawed and made illegal secondary or sympathy strike action and prevented unions in one sector, for example teachers, balloting in support of nurses or any other profession. The Act redefined what trade disputes were. The new definition of a trade dispute only applied to issues of pay and working conditions. Additionally, the new definition of a trade dispute only applied to issues of pay and working conditions. Secret ballots became a legal requirement under the Trade Union Act of 1984. For any strike to be legal, the balloting had to be secret, which meant that members could not be subjected to intimidation if they chose to vote against the position of their union. This was an important democratic move my the Thatcher administration.

The 1988 Employment Act protected workers who refused to strike from being punished and gave them the right not to be unjustly disciplined. Union members also had the right to bring complaints, the right to inspect unions accounting records and there was the appointment of a commissioner for the rights of trades union members. In a counterintuitive way, this act did not really limit the ability of trades unions: if anything, it helped them become more accountable, more democratic, and more transparent, and it forced trades union movement to operate as a legal entity rather than as a very powerful club which had few real checks and balances.

The 1990 Employment Act gave employers the right to dismiss workers when they took part in unofficial strike action. In addition, subsequent strike actions relating to that dismissal would also be unlawful. In 1992, the conservative government under John Major, introduced the Trade Union and Labour Relations Act which made it clear that unions must be recognised by an employer before legal industrial action could be taken. Irrespective of how many employees belong to a union, if the employer did not recognise the union, the employees would be unable to take industrial action.

The problems with unions for Friedman are that they have special immunities which provide them with the legal protection to engage in action which negatively affected society. Each person should be free to join or not to join a trade union, but the practice of unions preventing people from earning a decent income or preventing people getting jobs was to the detriment of society (Friedman: 1977,12). Friedman looked at the role of trades unions in Great Britain and he saw that their effect was more harmful in nationalised industry. For Hayek, socialism, or collectivism, ultimately leads to fascism. However, Hayek believed that socialists were, in their hearts, democrats, but that in order to realise the socialist dream, one would have to employ non-democratic methods of coercion, because planning leads to dictatorship, as dictatorship is the most efficient instrument of coercion (Hayek: 50). Individual liberty cannot be reconciled to a single societal purpose or aim, so in order to realise a single purpose, society must be subordinated and coerced. Hayek appeared to be blind sighted by the fact that this type of control and coercion could be invoked by the right as well as the left. It could well be argued that given the dominance of the conservatives and the political right in British politics, that the *New -and old - Right* has indeed exercised a disproportionate level of control, coercion and authoritarianism, evidenced by a quirk of democracy to choose the person or party who will wield absolute power.

Welfare and a Free Society

On the welfare state, Hayek commences his discussion by exploring how socialism had captured the minds of intellectual leaders who regarded socialism as the ultimate goal towards which society was inevitably moving (Hamowy: 2011,369).

Socialism was, for Hayek, an experiment that Britain undertook in earnest after the Second World War. The definitive aim of socialist movements was the nationalisation of the means of production, distribution, and exchange, so all economic activity would be directed toward addressing social injustice.

For Hayek, socialism had lost intellectual appeal and had been abandoned by the masses to such an extent that across the western world, socialism was searching for a new agenda that would gain it followers. Although the ultimate aim of socialism had not been abandoned, the methods socialists hoped to use to achieve their goal had largely been discredited because the socialism in Russia was not a model that others wanted to emulate or, indeed, live under. For Hayek, the Russian experience had led to less freedom for citizens; industry and businesses were less productive; hierarchy became more ingrained, and workers found themselves pitted against the state rather than individual employers, which created a significant imbalance of power and a threat to workers. Perhaps the most important factor in the disillusionment with socialism was the growing apprehension that socialism would herald the end of individual liberty. What was of importance for Hayek was that even though socialism had been generally abandoned as a goal to strive for, it was still possible to establish it unintentionally. Those reformers who focus on the most expedient path to achieve their purposes typically pay little or no attention to what is necessary to preserve an effective market mechanism, and they are therefore more likely to be led to impose central control over economic decisions until they unknowingly, and unintentionally arrive at a system of central planning that few wish to see established. Furthermore, many of the old socialists, according to Hayek, discovered that society was already drifting towards a redistributive state, and it was much easier to move in that direction than towards the discredited aim of centralising the means of production.

Hayek distinguished welfarism from socialism. The idea that government activity should be limited to the maintenance of law and order cannot be justified by the principles of liberty as discussed by Hayek. In his discussion, he says that only the coercive powers of government need to be strictly limited and that there is a wide berth for non-coercive activity to take place. No government in our modern times, he argued, confined itself to a minimum role, but all made provision for the unfortunate and disabled and concerned themselves with the question of health. Hayek sees no reason why the volume of these services should not increase with the growth of wealth in a nation (Hayek, 1960: 257). Common needs abound that can only be satisfied by collective action without restricting individual liberty. However, at times he saw that welfare provisions could be a threat to individual freedom because the services could constitute an exercise of government power and rested on them claiming exclusive rights in certain fields. In contrast, he sees the danger of socialism as of the collective kind because socialism would produce outcomes that were unwanted even by the proponents of socialism themselves. The same could not be said about the welfare state because the term did not rely upon a definitive system in order to operate but was a plethora of ideas and elements, some of which were compatible, while others were incompatible with a free society. The danger highlighted by Hayek was that once an aim of government becomes legitimate, it is assumed that even aims that run counter to the principles of a free society may be legitimately employed. The ambitious reformer who witnesses an evil and wishes to rid society of it will opt for a sudden and immediate abolition of that evil. What is to be guarded against is that their impatience to rid society of an evil could give the state exclusive and monopolistic powers. Care should be taken so that the state does not become paternalistic in its endeavours to impose levels and standards on individuals, taking away and depriving them of personal choice.

Hayek accepted without question the need for minimum public assistance, which should be sufficient to ensure food and shelter; but no more – to even the neediest. Beyond this point of subsistence provision, Hayek finds no objective standard to which policy could conform because individuals and groups will have their own ideas as to what resources they need. There is no standard above the subsistence line that can be upheld.

Hayek saw the welfare state as a form of society, or a set of institutions. He was opposed to such a configuration because it had the potential to threaten individual freedom. Who is to administer welfare benefits? Hayek argued against state monopolies and finance through distributive taxation. As the provider of the last resort, no other agency can protect people against the extremes of starvation and other circumstances beyond their control. A medical monopoly can guarantee the same level of service; however, progress depends on allowing people to seek out what they want. Hayek is not averse to monopoly or large organisations/corporations, only obstacles to entry into industries and certain monopolistic practises that are harmful. Monopoly is always undesirable, but only in the sense that scarcity of resources and goods are. Instead of state monopoly, reliance on personal, family, and occupational insurance is advocated. The state should require, that there is a minimum degree of protection for all, but the provision of that should not necessarily be with the state. Hayek does not point out how this subsistence level of resources is to be measured or what constitutes subsistence welfare, nor, indeed, who or what compendium of institutions and individuals decide.

Milton Friedman explained that even though the emphasis of socialist intellectuals had changed and that there was common agreement that widescale nationalisation was no longer desirable, the goal and threat to a free society remained. In a 1977 lecture, at the Swedish Bank in Stokholm, (Skandinaviska Enskilda Banken, (SEB) entitled, *The Fallacy of the Welfare State*,

Friedman argued that intellectuals had shifted away from traditional socialism toward a welfare state. Friedman argued that the drive to increase equality and achieve full employment had produced the welfare state and an expansive role for government, which was something that was at odds with what Marxists had originally wanted. In this lecture, Friedman explained that when good people try to do good things, they assumed that they knew better than the individuals for whom they were doing the good things on behalf of. He referenced Germany and Bismarck and that the first example in the Western world of extensive social welfare measures was instigated by Bismarck in the Prussian state, However, the way, and the form in which it was implemented in Britain was, in Friedman's mind, disastrous. During this speech, he made reference to the folly of Winston Churchill and how Churchill implemented social insurance and workers' pensions which kickstarted the welfare state (Freidman: 1977, 2-3). Friedman returned to the central thesis of Hayek, which was that in order to spend more money, the government had to take money forcibly from people. This was coercion, and a threat to a free society. The act of the state forcibly taking people's money meant that people would have less of their own money and conversely: they would ultimately want the money that the state took from them to be spent on themselves, which in-turn would create a disincentive to work and to provide for oneself.

In *Capitalism and Freedom* (1962), Friedman maintained that competitive capitalism, was the most efficient economic model because through the division of labour and specialisations, diverse needs could be met. Competitive capitalism was an example of proportional representation in the market place. There were however, limits; and competitive capitalism could not be extended to its logical conclusion, as this would lead to anarchy. Friedman maintained that on issues like policing and defence, there could be no proportional representation of interests like in the market, as it would lead to inefficiencies and fragmentation: these, therefore needed to be dealt with as political matters (Friedman, 1962. 23). He also argued that in relation to welfare provision when the free market operated effectively, voluntary arrangements would be sufficient to provide welfare assistance. Friedman drew reference to the United States of America and Great Britain In the 19th century and argued that the state played very little role. But people, through their voluntary activities and actions provided for each other. He sees that the challenge is how the state rolls back its involvement in welfare provision, but he saw that the rolling back was necessary, because one of the vices of the welfare state was that it destroyed private voluntary activity (Friedman: 1977). For Friedman, many areas of policy needed to be taken out of the political sphere and left to the market because, by its nature, politics was divisive and antagonistic. For Friedman, the government should leave the market to perform competitively and only act as the umpire, using the rule of law to regulate. If this is done, then both the *intrinsic value of economic freedom,* - which was about a multiplicity of products, services; specialisms; divisions of labour - and the *instrumental value of economic freedom,* - which required a decentralised economic system, dissimilar to that which occurs in many political systems where power is concentrated—would thrive.

This is where we begin to see Thatcherism's convergence and alignment with the Hayekian and Friedman doctrines of economic freedom, individuality and liberty juxtaposed to the political ideologies of socialism and collectivism, which were in opposition to free market competitive capitalism, individuality, and freedom from central control and coercion.

CHAPTER 5

Thatcher's Monetarism: Success or Failure

To some degree, it is unfair to see the failed monetarist programme that Mrs Thatcher sought to implement as representing a failure of monetarism. The rolling back of the state led to a period of severe recession with a quarter of British manufacturing companies closing down, and there was a huge slump in investment. Milton Friedman watched the decline in Britain with horror as the effect of the recession and failure in Britain was tarnishing his reputation in the USA. Friedman criticised Margaret Thatcher and explained that his version of capitalism had nothing to do with the size of government, taxation and spending, whether industries should be nationalised, the role of unions, or the fight against socialism. This was a significant intervention from Milton Friedman as he laid bare the areas of divergence between himself and Hayek and how Mrs Thatcher sought to apply the purer economics of Friedman to the political economics of Hayek. In this regard, Hayek's fight against socialism, collectivism and fascism is an example of where Margaret Thatcher had fused the economic and political ideology of Hayek with Friedman's monetarism, conservative authoritarianism and liberalism, creating a hybrid of economic and political ideology called Thatcherism.

Milton Friedman's monetarism was anchored in the relationship between the supply of money, prices, unemployment, and interest rates. One of his key criticisms of Margaret Thatcher's economic monetary policies was that she had reduced the supply of money too quickly whilst overall taxation remained high, inflation was inflating, companies were struggling to repay banks at higher interest rates, which also increased the supply of money in the economy; and unemployment was spiking. With unemployment increasing, there was a corresponding upsurge in the benefits bill and, by extension, an increase in public expenditure in the very areas of the economy that Thatcher's monetarism aimed to curtail. As a supply-side economist, one of the core tenants of monetarism is to control the supply of money and reduce taxation; none of these were done successfully by Mrs Thatcher. In fact, in 1987, Friedman wrote an open letter after learning that Mrs Thatcher had advised the US President and Congress that in order to stabilise the world economy, the US needed to reduce the federal government's budget deficit by imposing higher indirect taxes on a range of consumer goods. In his letter, Friedman explained, *'As one of your long-time admirers and supporters, I respectfully beg to differ. I believe that higher taxes of any kind, direct or indirect, are bad economics and even worse politics. Tax increases will harm, not benefit, the world's economy.* (Friedman: 1987).

Friedman went on, *'Higher taxes will not reduce the deficit, except for a brief interval. They will simply increase government spending. The desire of members of Congress to spend has been restrained by the existence of a large deficit. Higher taxes will, [however] permit higher spending without a higher government deficit. Higher spending means that the government will command a larger fraction of the nation's resources and private individuals a smaller fraction. That is not a result I would expect you to favour'*. Like Hayek, Friedman believed that currency should be freed from certain constraints, and in this open letter, yhwh be praised, Mrs Thatcher, saying, *'One of your major achievements on becoming Prime Minister was to end foreign exchange control and to set the pound free'*. At the end of his open letter, he concluded, *'Let me urge you to consider whether the advice you have given is truly consistent with your strong and principled support of voluntary co-*

operation of free people in free markets, with a minimum of government intervention' (Friedman: 1987).

In her understandable urgency to reduce inflation and grow the British economy, Margaret Thatcher acted in haste with an insufficient understanding of how to apply, and the possible effects of misapplying Hayek and Friedman. She had cut and pasted what she thought were the main components of the monetarism of Friedman and the social liberal free market economics of Hayek. It is undoubtedly the case that this was more about politics and sending political signals - that her government was going to be strong on the economy, strong against the unions, and strong about unleashing individual autonomy - than it was about economics. This is the inevitable Faustian pact that many politicians sign up for or are subjected to. On the one hand, they want to do the best for the country and the economy; on the other hand, they are either constrained or unleashed by the various wings of their political party; on the third hand, they may be beholden to sectional interests: all of whom inevitably want the arch of decisions to inexorably bend in their favour; and on the fourth hand, we must not forget that the personal pride and hubris of politicians play a major role in their need to be revered and remembered. Both then and now, it was clear that the Thatcher government was adopting a hard ideological position on the economy, public expenditure, privatisation, and trades unions. It is even clearer now that her preoccupation with politicking meant that there was an insufficient appreciation of the intricate nature of the British economy, the world economy, and the interconnectedness of pulling the wrong levers of monetary policy resulted in a deep recession.

Thatcherism and The Return of (Enoch) Powellism

With the ascension of Margaret Thatcher to the leadership of the conservative party, the One Nation programme dwindled into insignificance, and the drive for greater individuality, choice, and economic growth took precedence. The *New Right* - which Margaret Thatcher represented - was a powerful counter-revolution designed to eradicate socialism in favour of a radical return to 19th century liberalism. The wealthy, the privileged, and the well-apportioned were always destined to win as they had acquired, or retained advantageous financial, familial, economic, social and other important links and connections whether historically through colonial Britain, or through 'relatively' new wealth. For this cohort, a competitive market would never diminish their gains, or their advantage. What Mrs Thatcher dared to do, however, was to give a little bit of the pie to the masses. The resultant effect, whether by design or accident was to stop widespread descent while reducing public spending for those who would always require it and for whom, irrespective of how hard they worked, they would remain financially in the lower quartile of society. This was an example of the populist politician who also had a strong authoritarian streak as displayed in the way that she handled the striking miners, teaching them a lesson after the way they had undermined Edward Heath's conservative government.

With the backdrop of economic decline; the defeat of the Conservative Party in two elections in 1974; the 1974 and '79 collapse of price and incomes policies; high interest rates and high inflation in 1975; trades union strikes, and the winter of discontent, created such a level of discomfort and disillusionment in the country. The political left and the Labour Party doubled down on their commitment to state ownership; Keynesian intervention; full employment, and Britain's withdrawal from the European Economic Community. The country needed something new, something different: this came in the personification of Margaret Thatcher and her *New Right* project.

Thatcherism was a British version of the new social, economic, and political ideology that had been sweeping across the United States and western Europe. This new approach promised growth and prosperity by focusing responsibility from the state and onto the individual as an answer to the economic problems of the 1970s in Europe and America. Margaret Thatcher, as a politician wanted seismic change and needed a new credible social and economic framework with which to encase her beliefs. When she found that free market economics and monetarism, provided that, she was willing to implement them with a sharp eye on political and economic pragmatism.

The economist and philosopher Adam Smith was a central figure for Thatcherism and the *New Right*. Margaret Thatcher subscribed to the Smithsonian view that the chief design of every system of government was the maintenance of justice. In a position redolent of conservatism, Adam Smith saw the role of government as being to preserve what each individual had acquired; for Smith, commercial society was the best form of society to realise that. Smith accepted that within a commercial society, the pursuit of wealth and power generated inequality; however, for him, inequality was a necessary by-product. At the heart of the *New Right* brand of conservatism was the notion that competition and the market would provide opportunities for all and that each individual could grow and needn't remain in poverty. For Smith, inequality was the result of imprudent living and he argued that a rich man's wealth came from prudence as a rich man could eat no more than a poor man (Smith:1784, 10). Smith believed that as the wealth of all increased, people would be able to pursue the full range of moral values open to all and act justly, and a just society was the only society that presented the opportunity for good morals and civil life. As time went on, Smith realised that capitalism had an interest in deceiving the public and that capitalism would attempt to distort the market in its favour. Due to these and other negative factors, society acted against economic growth and the condition of the poor. Smith wanted a minimalist and less interventionist state whose primary economic duty was to maintain the freedom of the market (Smith:1784). Milton Friedman, who also greatly influenced Margaret Thatcher and the *New Right* also saw the importance of economic freedom, as this freedom would allow a multiplicity of diverse products and services to proliferate in the market, allowing/enabling diverse needs to be met.

Thatcherism was rooted in the traditional conservatism of the 18th century and the liberalism of the 19th century and it was able to bring about a conflation of liberalism and conservatism. Liberalism in the market place was anchored in the pre-eminence of the individual over the collective, and aimed to foster a culture of enterprise. Conservatism provided the ideology that justified public policy outcomes in terms of restoring traditional conservative values, a belief in a strong state in terms of law, order, God and responsibility. Hayek however, rejected the conflation of liberalism and conservatism as he believed that conservatives in Britain were resistant to free market ideas; they, be praised, favoured a strong expanding government; they were hostile to internationalism (as Winston Churchill found); and they had nationalist tendencies.

Mrs Thatcher set about rolling back the powers of the state by attempting to lessen the input and influence of those who, in the Hayekian sense were planners, seeking to orchestrate and coercively plan the economy. Her response was to relinquish centralised control and management by using central markets to break the monopoly control of service providers/suppliers. Central government, local government, their employers, and trades unions were to lose power, and consumers, voters, ratepayers, and tenants were to gain power. In this move towards decentralisation, the government was forced to operate in a very different way and it paradoxically became more centralised as it gathered increased power to itself. The rational belief was that in order to rejuvenate the economy and facilitate a private sector-led recovery, public expenditure had to be cut, but only a powerful/strong government would be able to undertake this. Securing greater power was antithetical to a reform agenda aimed at creating a less powerful and less intrusive government. However, the government argued that greater involvement of the private sector and privatisation would ultimately roll back the power of the state and the public sector without diminishing the powers of the government, or parliament to exercise oversight and accountability through regulation, standards, and codes of conduct.

However, the effectiveness of that oversight ability and regulatory capacity and capability exercised by the government, its various agencies and parliament over the last 30 years have been brought into question. There has been numerous examples of companies and organisations engaged in delivering services to citizens circumventing regulations and codes of conduct and have seemingly operated with impunity. Adam Smith was aware of this potential and explained that, if left to its own devices, capitalism's self-interest would see it deceiving the public and attempting to distort the market in its favour. Examples of this include the contaminated blood scandal in the 1970s and 1980s where 4,689 people with Haemophilia and other bleeding disorders were infected with HIV and Hepatitis viruses; the rolling back of regulation which preceded the 2008 banking crisis; the mis-selling of payment protection insurance in the financial services industry; the poor maintenance of our water infrastructure and the routine dispersal of sewage into our rivers; the charging and pricing structures of electricity, energy, water, and train companies; the 30-year Windrush immigration scandal, and the 20-year Post Office Horizon scandal which was the largest miscarriage of justice in UK history, where over 700 Post Masters and Mistresses were convicted and some sent to prison for fraud due to Fujitsu's Horizon software. These and other failures were not all due to companies running rogue; in many instances, there were failures of regulators to regulate and of governments via ministers and select committees to bring bad and malpractice to account.

While processes and procedures have been established to bring about accountability, irrespective of the distance: in reality, actual accountability has become even more difficult to attain.

For proponents of the free market like Hayek, the individual is the starting point and the end of any analysis of human behaviour, and the market is best placed to reflect the intricate pattern of supply and demand; hence, whatever individuals require, the market will provide and individuals will be willing to purchase those goods at an agreeable price. However, as we know, as a result of the policies implemented by Mrs Thatcher, the reality was that many people fell below the poverty line and inequality increased. Despite this being a potential outcome, both Margaret Thatcher, and Hayek saw the creation and maintenance of a welfare state as an infringement to individual autonomy and freedom and as a planned intervention that was designed to alter the workings of the market. For them, the welfare state could be surpassed by the market, and the market could provide goods based on the demand of the customer.

Government intervention was therefore always undesirable because its intervention altered the mechanisms of a market that was too complex to be controlled, and for Hayek, it inevitably involved coercion and a lack of freedom.

Hayek lauded free markets because, without them, personal liberty, property rights, and the rule of law were not possible. For Friedman, the *New Right*, and Mrs Thatcher, competitive capitalism and free markets enabled the highest form of freedom and individual liberty. Keynesians and those on the political left disagreed fundamentally that the market was largely benign and a pure catalyst for freedom. What those on the political left could not ignore however, was the historical evidence that competitive free market economies tended to produce more wealth than socialist and collectivist systems. The left attacked free markets on the grounds of morals, greed, selfishness, and an awareness that, left unchecked, competitive free markets would perpetuate the divisions between Disraeli's two nations and ingrain the inequality between those who have - by virtue of birth and circumstances - and those who do not.

The recurrent theme interwoven in Hayek and in Thatcherism was liberty and responsibility, which meant individuals were free to pursue and make choices, the consequences of which they must be willing to accept. For Hayek, liberty and responsibility were inseparable, and a free society would not function or maintain itself unless each citizen saw it as their duty to accept that the position they found themselves in was due to their own actions. In a free society, individuals are given the opportunity to make use of the available resources, and since no one can know, or dictate the degree to which each individual has, or can do this, it should be left to individuals to pursue their own aims.

Margaret Thatcher and the *New Right* undoubtedly agreed with Hayek's assertion that the freedom to pursue one's own aims free from a coercive state was of preeminent importance. Milton Friedman, in arguing for competitive capitalism, maintained that government was necessary to preserve economic freedom, but concentrating power in political hands was also a potential threat to the intrinsic value of economic freedom. For the most altruistic person, as for the most egotist and self-centred person, the chief concern is the welfare of their families, and altruism, generally applied, was a meaningless concept because no one could effectively care for other people because the responsibility we will assume will always be particular and focused on those who we know. For Adam Smith, this was at the heart of his argument that self-love was the force that drove the market system, and it was unreasonable to expect people to act benevolently, but they would act for the benefit of all if they could see their own advantages (Smith: 1784). This individualism and self-interest were at the heart of Thatcherism and her policies, the budgets of her chancellors demonstrated the extent of Mrs Thatcher's commitment to the monetarism of Milton Friedman and the free market libertarianism of Friedrich Von Hayek.

Rhetoric and reality are frequently at odds, and in the 1980s the *New Right* did not have a homogeneous ideology that its proponents collectively adhered to. What they had was a somewhat simplistic analysis of society along with policies that aimed to provide choice through competition, offering to replace the state-run demoralised welfare state with the modus operandi of a progressive market economy that would supposedly give freedom and access to all. Thatcherism and the *New Right* promulgated the idea that liberty and equality were incompatible because equality meant taking from some to give to others. The Thatcherite answer to this, was for the government to give something to the citizen; not take something away from other citizens. Her master stroke was to give those in council houses, the right to purchase their council houses. Her second masterstroke was that, with privatisation, ordinary people were able to buy shares in newly privatised utilities. These two actions propelled Thatcherism along.

Hayek provided the economic and political framework that Thatcherism and the *New Right* so much needed. Both aligned and subscribed to Hayek's fears that, left unchecked; socialism and collectivism in Britain would lead inexorably to coercion and an inevitable slide into fascism. Rolling back the state and enabling the free market to run its course was a protection against the inevitability of coercion. Along with the monetarism of Milton Friedman, Margaret Thatcher amalgamated the pragmatic and somewhat contradictory positions of Hayek and Friedman into her unique blend of Thatcherism.

Milton Friedman publicly disassociated himself from the approach and the unfolding results of Margaret Thatcher. Hayek, - writing pre-emptively - was aware that people would assume that he was a conservative, so he distanced himself from that association in the postscript of *The Constitution of Liberty*: '*Why I Am Not a Conservative*'. Hayek explained in this postscript that he was not a conservative because the Conservative Party of Great Britain was resistant to free market ideas, favoured a strong, expanding government and had tendencies to authoritarianism. This propensity to close ranks and the resistance to free trade were amongst the issues that compelled Winston Churchill to leave the conservative party and join the Liberals in 1904. In 2024, in the context of Brexit, the culture wars and the inflammatory comments and statements by the former Home Secretary, Suella Braverman, and other members of the conservative party, it appears that the perceived insularity of the conservative party is an enduring faulty gene. It was prescient that Hayek, writing in 1960, also saw then, that the Conservative Party of Great Britain was hostile to internationalism and prone to nationalism. Hayek also rejected the idea that he was a conservative because the Conservative Party had welcomed collectivism and found some common ground with socialism. The conservative party had a *'...fear of change, a timid distrust of the new... conservatives are inclined to use the powers of government to prevent change or to limit its rate to whatever appeals to the more timid mind... [conservatives have a] fondness for authority and [a] lack of understanding of economic forces'* (Hayek: 2011, 522). In a sharp criticism of the conservatives, Hayek stated that *'Like the socialist, [the conservative] is less concerned with the problem of how the powers of government should be limited than with ... who wields them; and, like the socialist, [the conservative] regards [themselves] as entitled to force the values [they] hold on other people* (Hayek: 2011, 522-533). These were the reasons he was not a conservative.

There were undoubtedly real-life political, social, and economic challenges that stymied or restrained the Thatcher government's ability to roll out Hayek's and Friedman's free market, competitive capitalist monetarist theories. It should also not be dismissed that many of the *New Right* and Thatcherites had not fully understood Hayek and Friedman economics and were professing something that they had heard, or surmised at the time.

Margaret Thatcher, through Thatcherism has become the benchmark for the conservative party and conservative party leaders. The left of politics has not been inured to the Thatcher effect; and there have been those, who having adopted Thatcherite policies and have welcomed being seen/anointed as heirs of Thatcherism, whilst others have sought to distinguish themselves as the antithesis of all that she stood for.

Margaret Thatcher was, and will remain a hugely consequential figure in British politics. She was a pragmatist and never really set out to implement monetarism in its truest form. Although she was wedded to the free market, and subscribed to the economic solutions proffered by Friedrich Von Hayek, Thatcherism lost its way when faced with the reality of the real world. As Mike Tyson famously said, *'everyone has a plan until they get punched in the mouth'*.

Mrs Thatcher has been variously described as a Hayekian and as a follower of Milton Friedman, but based on what she did, and its effects; Friedman distanced himself from her. Writing in earlier times, and as discussed in earlier chapters, Hayek disassociated himself from conservatives. What is clear, is that Thatcherism was an ideology, and it had a plan. If today's politicians have no ideas for the future, they will look to the past: and as we know: the past is a foreign country and in a different time.

Margaret Thatcher was a failed Hayekian and a failed monetarist; but she was the most successful Thatcherite that there ever was; and ever will be.

An Eye to the Future

Over the last fourteen years, a Conservative government, - who for a short period of time were in coalition with the liberal democrats - has been in power in the United Kingdom. Over that period of time, life in the United Kingdom has become harder with incomes trailing behind the cost of living; international and local price increases on staple products and services; increasingly unpredictable and higher inflation; inefficiencies and reduced access to public services, and of course, the additional increase in costs associated with Britain leaving the European Union. Despite the narrative that conservative governments are historically competent at managing the economy, from the time that David Cameron and George Osborne took the reins of power, they presided over real-terms cuts in capital expenditure, and refused to borrow at a time when interest rates for government borrowing was at an historic low. In contrast, the cuts in public expenditure that Margaret Thatcher implemented, were not real-term cuts as the retrenchment in capital expenditure were largely mitigated and off-set by the considerable revenues that flowed into the UK Treasury from North Sea oil.

The effects of David Cameron's and George Osborne's austerity has been the diminution in the ability of public services to deliver adequate services. That lack of delivery has been compounded by a lack of effective, statutory, or regulatory accountability, despite numerous reports by the House of Commons, Public Accounts Select Committee raising concerns and calling for improvements.

When the conservative-led Liberal Democrat coalition government came to power in 2010, they agreed that deficit reduction was their priority. At the time, national debt was £1.03

trillion and grew to £1,663.0 billion by the end of 2015. From April to June 2023, the UK government's gross debt was £2,636.9 trillion, equivalent to 101.2% of gross domestic product (GDP) (ONS: 2024). It is true that COVID had an impact on this; however, before COVID, at the end of December 2020, government gross debt was £2,206.5 trillion. So, Covid added £430.4 billion to the debt. It is clear that under the conservatives, the national debt has risen alarmingly, and the country has been further impoverished.

Arguably, in an attempt to obscure and ignore the effects of austerity, the current economic record, and the disaster of the premierships of Liz Truss and Rishi Sunak, the modern conservative party appears to have abandoned the political middle ground and is unapologetically occupying, and fighting on nationalistic right-wing and, to some extent, far right-wing issues.

As discussed earlier, there is precedent for this. The nationalism, anti-trade and parochialism that caused Winston Churchill to abandon the conservative party and cross the floor to join the Liberal Party was also evident to Hayek. Friedrich von Hayek rejected conservatism because he feared that the conservatives were more *concerned with wielding power, forcing their values on other people*, and had unattractive nationalistic tendencies. The fears of Winston Churchill and Hayek has continued to simmer in the bosom of the party and it has resurfaced stronger than ever. Right wing nationalism and inward facing ideologies have been breastfed, nurtured and has been flexing its baby muscles. In part, the conservative party's preoccupation with Britain's Exit (BREXIT) from the European Union was a symptom of this.

The conservative party is in self-preservation mode and appears to be fighting to retain power, for its own sake.

It is intriguing that in the 21st century, thanks to David Cameron, diversity and inclusion in the Conservative Party has seen it jump ahead of the Labour Party on key metrics of diversity and inclusion. The conservative party has not stopped there, but it has welcomed a plethora of diverse people into senior positions as chairmen, leader and prime ministers. There is however, a high degree of cognitive dissonance, in that these diverse members of the party are espousing a form of nationalism which sees people who look like them, as no longer desirable in the United Kingdom. The next iteration of the conservative party; if it survives as a distinct entity; is highly likely to be in the image of Enoch Powell.

BIBLIOGRAPHY

Addison, P. (1992) Churchill On The Home Front 1900-1955, p.207 (London: Jonathan Cape)

Addison, Paul. (1993) 'Churchill and Social Reform' in Robert Blake and William Roger Louis (eds), Churchill (Oxford, Oxford University Press), p.60

Bateman, B.W. (1987). Keynes's Changing Conception of Probability, Economics and Philosophy, 3, 97-120

BBC (2013) The Thatcher Years in Statistics. Accessed 1 March 2024 https://www.bbc.co.uk/news/uk-politics-22070491

Bean, C. Symons, J. (1989) Ten Years of Mrs T. URL: http://www.nber.org/chapters/c10962 p. 13 – 72. In Blanchard, O. and Fischer, S. ED NBER Macroeconomics Annual (1989) Volume 4, MIT Press http://www.nber.org/books/blan89-1

Boyson, R (1978) Centre Forward A radical Conservative programme. London Temple Smith

Braggion, Fabio. Narly Dwarkasing, and Lyndon Moore (2012) "From Competition to Cartel: Bank Mergers in the UK 1885 to 1925." Tilburg University. 10.2139/ssrn.1548828. SSRN Electronic Journal

Brewer, M and Wernham, T (2022) Wealth is the Growing Economic Divide in the UK today. Institute For Fiscal Studies Accessed 19th December 2023 [https://ifs.org.uk/news/wealth-growing-economic-divide-uk-today]

Capie, F and Billings. M. (2004) "Evidence on Competition in English Commercial Banking, 1920–1970." Financial History Review 11 (1): 69-103

Carabelli, A. (1988). On Keynes's Method. Macmillan

Chamber of Commerce (1918) Chamber Of Commerce Luncheon, Dundee, 10 December 1918. Accessed 5 December 2023 [https://winstonchurchill.org/publications/finest-hour/finest-hour-153/wit-and-wisdom-churchills-1918-yen-to-nationalize/]

Churchill, W, S. (1948) The Sinews of Peace: Post-War Speeches (London: Cassell)

Churchill, Randolph S. (1969) Winston S. Churchill, Companion, vol. ii, Part 2, 1907-1911, p. 861. London, Heinemann

Cmnd 7841. March 1980 Public Expenditure White Paper

Conservative Central Office (1976) The Right Approach A STATEMENT OF CONSERVATIVE AIMS. London [https://www.margaretthatcher.org/document/109439] Accessed 1st November 2023

Conservative Party Manifesto (1979) Accessed 4 January 2024 [http://www.conservativemanifesto.com/1979/1979-conservative-manifesto.shtml] Copyright © 2001 PoliticalStuff.co.uk.

Damond Commission (1974) Royal Commission on the Distribution of Incomes and Wealth, (1974-1979)

Davis, J.B. (1994). Keynes's Philosophical Development. Cambridge University Press

Dennison, S. R. (1959) "The British Restrictive Trade Practices Act of 1956." Journal of Law and Economics 2: 64-83

Department of Health (1989) Working for Patients. CM 555. London: HMSO.

Employment Gazette, February 1983 Vol. 91, Table 2.8

Environment Committee (1980) First report from the Environment Committee, session 1979-80: enquiry into implications of government's expenditure plans 1980-81 to 1983-84 for the housing policies of the Department of the Environment: together with the proceedings of the committee, the minutes of evidence and appendices.1980, H.M.S.O. Accessed 9th November 2023 [https://openlibrary.org/books/OL22707490M/First_report_from _the_Environment_Committee_session_1979-80]

Fitzgibbons, A. (1988). Keynes's Vision: A New Political Economy. Clarendon Press

Friedman M. (1980) Free to Choose. Published USA Harcourt and Brace Jovanovitch

Friedman, M (1962) Capitalism and Freedom. University of Chicago Press

Friedman, M. (1977) The Fallacy of the Welfare State. From The Collected Works of Milton Friedman, compiled and edited by Robert Leeson and Charles G. Palm. [https://miltonfriedman.hoover.org/internal/media/dispatcher/2 14521/full#:~:text=FRIEDMAN%3A%20No%2C%20I%20do%20not ,a%20minimum%20role%20of%20government] Accessed 23 March 2024

Friedman, M. (1987) An Open Letter from Milton Friedman to Margaret Thatcher. Financial Times (London), 4 December 1987 [https://miltonfriedman.hoover.org/internal/media/dispatcher/2 14966/full]

Friedman, M. (1993) Why Government is the Problem. * Essays in Public Policy, no. 39. Stanford, California: Hoover Institution Press. Accessed

[https://www.hoover.org/sites/default/files/uploads/documents/friedman-government-problem-1993.pdf]

Friedman, M. and Friedman, R. (1990) Free To Choose. [edition unavailable]. HarperCollins. Available at: https://www.perlego.com/book/3184365/free-to-choose-a-personal-statement-pdf (Accessed: 25 February 2023).

Gamble, A. (1974) The Conservative Nation, Routledge and Kegan Paul, London

Garrison, R. and Barr, N. (2014) Elgar Companion To Hayekian Economics. Edward Elgar Publishing Limited

Gillies, D. (2003) Probability and uncertainty in Keynes's general theory. University College London Accessed [https://discovery.ucl.ac.uk/id/eprint/16387/1/16387.pdf] 17th January 2024

Government Expenditure Plans 1983-84 to 1985-86, (1983) presented by Chancellor of the Exchequer, Cmnd. 8789, Vol. 1. P6: HMSO

Graham Hutton (1961) Agenda For A Free Society. In Individual and Society. London. Hutchinson and Co.

Hall, S. & Jacques, M. (1990) (Ed) New Times: the Changing Face of Politics in the 1990s. Lawrence & Wishart in association with Marxism Today. London

Hall, S. (1980) Popular-Democratic vs Authoritarian-Populism: Two Ways of Taking Democracy Seriously. In Hunt, A Ed. Marxism and Democracy. Publisher, Lawrence & Wishart

Hamowy, R. (Ed) (2011) The Collected Works of F.A Hayek Volume XVii. The Constitution Of Liberty. The Definitive Edition. Chicago Press

Hansard (1983) Council House Sales. Volume 51 cc426-8: debated on 21 December 1983.

Hansard HC (1979) Budget Statement Volume 968 [968/235-264]: Debated on Tuesday 12 June https://hansard.parliament.uk/Commons/1979-06-12/debates/29201248-ba1f-4cd1-b814-da4e5f064ece/CommonsChamber#main-content [Accessed 2nd November 2023

Hansard, (1944) HC Deb 21 June 1944 vol 401 cc211-310. Ernest Bevin introduces the White Paper on Employment policy, June 1944

Hayek, F A. (1939) Profits, Interest and Investment and Other Essays On The Theory Of Industrial Fluctuations. Publishers; Augustus M Kelley [Accessed 28th February 2024. https://cdn.mises.org/Profits,%20Interest,%20and%20Investment_5.pdf

Hayek, F A. (1972) A Tiger by the Tail. Third Edition. The Institute of Economic Affairs

Hayek, F. (1973/76/79) Law, Legislation, and Liberty, in 3 volumes, Chicago: University of Chicago Press

Hayek, F. 1960) The Constitution of Liberty. Chicago Press

Hayek, F. A. (1945) The Use of Knowledge in Society. The American Economic Review, Vol.35, No.4. (Sep.1945), pp.519-530. https://www.jstor.org/stable/1809376

Hayek, F.A. (1949) The Intellectuals and Socialism Reprinted from The University of Chicago Law Review (Spring 1949), pp. 417-420, 421-423, 425-433

Hayek, F.A. (1960) Constitution of Liberty. Published London, Routledge and Kegan Paul

Hayek, F.A. (1976) Choice in Currency: A Way to Stop Inflation https://iea.org.uk/publications/research/choice-in-currency-a-way-to-stop-inflation

Hayek, F.A. (1978) New Studies in Philosophy, Politics, Economics and the History of Ideas. The Errors of Constructivism. London: Routledge & Kegan Paul

Hayek, F.A. (2000) Road to Serfdom, Routledge; 2nd edition

Hayek, F.A. (2011) The Constitution of Liberty. University of Chicago Press, London

Hayek, F.A. Full Employment At Any Price? (1975) Fourth impression, Published by Tonbridge Kent, by, first published by IEA p5 Occasional Paper 45

HC (1981) Council House Rents HC Deb 16 December 1981 vol 15 cc362-402. [https://api.parliament.uk/historic-hansard/commons/1981/dec/16/council-house-rents] Accessed 9th November 2023.

Horn, K. I. (2009) Roads to Wisdom, Conversations with Ten Nobel Laureates in Economics. Edward Elgar Publishing

Howe, D. (1982) Conservatism In the Eighties. Published; Conservative Political Centre

Hunter, L. (1975) British Incomes Policy 1972 - 1974. ILR Review, Volume 29, No 1 (Oct 1975), pp67-88. Published by Sage publications Inc.

IEA. (1976/1977) Institute of Economic Affairs Choice in Currency. A Way to Stop Inflation. London: (Occasional Paper 48), February

Industrial Relations White Paper ('In Place of Strife', Cmnd 3888): ministerial briefing notes and discussion on policy for industrial relations. 1968 Jan 01 - 1969 Dec 31

Irvine, A. (2020) What Were the Key Causes of the Russian Revolution? Accessed 1 March 2024. https://www.historyhit.com/WHAT-WERE-THE-KEY-CAUSES-OF-THE-RUSSIAN-REVOLUTION/

Jenkins, R. (2001) Churchill. Macmillan

Jessop B, Bonnett K, Bromley S, Ling T, 1988 Thatcherism: A Tale of Two Nations (Polity Press, Cambridge)

Jessop et al: (1989) Thatcherism: A Tale Of Two Nations

Joseph, K. (1974) Speech at Preston Inflation is Caused by Governments. Accessed 12th January 2024 [https://www.margaretthatcher.org/document/110607]

Jukes, G. (2014) The Russo-Japanese War 1904–1905. Bloomsbury Publishing

Kavanagh, D. (1990) Thatcherism and British Politics. Oxford University Press

Kavanagh, D. (1990) Thatcherism and British Politics. The end of consensus? Oxford University Press, New York

Keynes, J M. (1919) The Economic Consequences of the Peace. (London: Macmillan

Keynes, J M. (1921), A Treatise on Probability, repr. 1973, The collected writings of John Maynard Keynes, vol. 8 (London: Macmillan for the Royal Economic Society). [Accessed 27th February 2024 [https://etheses.lse.ac.uk/2852/1/U615801.pdf]

Keynes, J M. (2009) The General Theory of Employment, Interest and Money. Pub Classic Books America. First Edition printed by Macmillan 1936

Lawson, N. (1984) Mais Lecture [https://www.margaretthatcher.org/document/109504] Accessed 25th October 2023

Lawson, T. and Pesaran, H. (Eds.) (1985). Keynes' Economics. Methodological Issues. Croom Helm

Lewis, P. Ed (2022) The Collected Works of F. A. Hayek Essays on Liberalism and the Economy, Volume 18

Leys, C. (1989) Politics in Britain From Labourism to Thatcherism. University of Toronto Press

LONGDEN, G. (1952) Powell to Longden, 20 October 1952, LONGDEN 4/1, Longden Papers

Marr, A. (2007) A History of Modern Britain. Pan

Marshall, C. and Porion, S. (2023) One Nation Conservatism from Disraeli to Johnson. Published CRECIB - Centre de recherche et d'études en civilisation britannique

Middleton, R (2000) The British Economy Since 1945. Palgrave Macmillan

Miller, E. (2010) Hayek's The Constitution of Liberty; An Account of his Argument. Institute of Economic Affairs (IEA)

Ministry Of Ways and Communications Bill Volume 35: debated on Monday 21 July 1919 [https://hansard.parliament.uk/Lords/1919-07-21/debates/1a9f86e5-2334-4c3d-9aae-44d304744967/MinistryOfWaysAndCommunicationsBill?highlight=unprecedented]

Moore, C. (2013) Margaret Thatcher. The Authorised Biography. Volume. Not For Turning. Allen Lane

Nobel (1974) The Sveriges Riksbank Prize in Economic Sciences in Memory of Alfred Nobel 1974. Friedrich von Hayek Prize Lecture NobelPrize.org. Nobel Prize Outreach AB 2023. Accessed Wed. 20 Sep 2023. https://www.nobelprize.org/prizes/economic-sciences/1974/hayek/lecture/

O'Donnell, R.M. (1989). Keynes: Economics, Philosophy and Politics. Macmillan

Office for National Statistics (2022) Consumer price inflation, historical estimates and recent trends, UK: 1950 to 2022

ONS: (2021) Long-term trends in UK employment: 1861 to 2018 [Accessed 15th November 2023. [https://www.ons.gov.uk/economy/nationalaccounts/uksectoraccounts/compendium/economicreview/april2019/longtermtrendsinukemployment1861to2018#trends-of-the-employment-rate]

ONS: (2024) Office for National Statistics. UK Government Debt and Deficit Statistical Bulletins Quarterly estimates of UK government debt and deficit. Accessed [January 19th 2024

Pimlott, B. Kavanagh, D. & Morris, P. (1989) Is the 'postwar consensus' a myth? Contemporary Record, 2:6, 12-15, DOI: 10.1080/13619468908581025

Plant, R. (2009) The Neo-Liberal State: Oxford University Press

Porion, S. (2023) Enoch Powell's Contribution Within the One Nation Group (1950-1955): Towards a Proto-Thatcherite Appropriation of One Nation Conservatism", Revue Française de Civilisation Britannique [Online], XXVIII-1 DOI: https://doi.org/10.4000/rfcb.10488

Randolph S. Churchill, Winston S. Churchill, Companion (London, Heinemann 1969), vol. ii, Part 2, 1907-1911, p. 861

Rose, R. (1985) Politics in England. Table. Changes in Programmes of Public Expenditure 1953-1973 (as percent of total public spending). London Faber

Runde, J. (1994). Keynes After Ramsey: In Defence of A Treatise on Probability, Studies in History and Philosophy of Science, 25 (1), 97-121

Schmidtz, D and Boettke, P. (2021) "Friedrich Hayek", The Stanford Encyclopedia of Philosophy (Summer 2021 Edition), Edward N. Zalta (ed.).
[https://plato.stanford.edu/archives/sum2021/entries/friedrich-hayek/]

Schumpeter, J. (1942) Capitalism, Socialism, and Democracy. Published by Harper & Brothers)

Scmidtz, David and Peter Boettke. (2001) 'Friedrich Von Hayek', The Stanford Encyclopaedia of Philosophy (Summer 2021 Edition), Edward N. Zalta (ed).
[https://plato.stanford.edu/archives/sum2021/entries/friedrich-hayek] (2021) Publisher Metaphysics Research Lab, Stanford University

Sewell, R. (2003) In the Cause of Labour - A History of British Trade Unionism

Shearmur, J. (2006). Hayek, The Road to Serfdom, and the British Conservatives. Journal of the History of Economic Thought, 28(3), 309-314. doi:10.1080/10427710600857807

Skidelsky, R. (1983). John Maynard Keynes. Vol. 1. Hopes Betrayed 1883-1920. Macmillan

Skidelsky, R. (1992). John Maynard Keynes. Vol 2. The Economist as Saviour 1920-1937. Macmillan

Skidelsky, R. (2000). John Maynard Keynes. Vol.3. Fighting for Britain 1937-1946. Macmillan

Skidelsky, R. (2009) Keynes: The Return of the Master. Allen Lane pp. 116, 126

Smith, A. (1784) The Wealth of Nations. The first edition was published in 1776, I have accessed the 1784 edition

Sotiropoulos, D P. Milios, J. and Lapatsioras (2013) A Political Economy of Contemporary Capitalism and its Crisis. Demystifying finance. Routledge

Thatcher, M (1979) Speech to the Conservative Political Centre Summer School ("The Renewal of Britain") Accessed 1 February 2024 [https://www.margaretthatcher.org/document/104107]

Thatcher, M (1989) The Revival of Britain. Speech to the Conservative Party conference at Blackpool, 10th of October 1975. London, Arum Press p27

Thatcher, M. (1995b) The Path To Power. Harper Collins

Thatcher. M. (1975a) Speech to the Institute of Socio-Economic Studies ("Let Our Children Grow Tall") September [https://www.margaretthatcher.org/document/102769] Accessed 2nd November 2023

Thatcher. M. (1975c) Speech to Conservative Party Conference. October. Blackpool [https://www.margaretthatcher.org/document/102777]

UK Finance. (2023) Mortgage Arrears and Possessions Update Quarter 3

White, Lawrence H, (1999). "Hayek's Monetary Theory and Policy: A Critical Reconstruction," Journal of Money, Credit and Banking, Blackwell Publishing, vol. 31(1), pages 109-120, February

Williamson, N. (1984) New Right Men Behind Mrs Thatcher. Spokesman Books

Wood, J (1970) Powell and the 1970 Election. Kingswood, Surrey, Elliot Right Way Books

INDEX

A
Adam Smith · 8, 23, 72, 101, 139, 141, 144
Alfred Sherman · 61, 101
Anthony Barber · 53
Authoritarianism · 5, 12, 14, 92, 135, 145

B
Bank of England · 28, 64
Beveridge · 38, 51, 52
Bloody Sunday · 18
Brexit · 35

C
Chancellor · 33, 38, 39, 53, 59, 79, 89, 101, 126
Churchill · 5, 31, 32, 36, 37, 38, 39, 40, 41, 42, 44, 46, 47, 82, 140, 145
Coercion · 5, 12, 21, 29, 61, 97, 99, 120, 121, 124, 125, 129, 143, 145
Cold War · 19
Common Market · 62
Competition · 22, 26, 41, 44, 52, 55, 56, 62, 63, 72, 84, 85, 95, 105, 111, 122, 124, 139, 144
Competitive Markets · 21

Conservative Government · 32, 43, 44, 59, 75, 84, 87, 88, 102, 138

Conservative Party · 1, 3, 4, 5, 31, 34, 40, 41, 52, 64, 65, 75, 81, 97, 104, 138, 145
Corn Laws · 35
Council Houses · 3, 145

D
David Cameron · 5
Democracy · 58, 64, 67, 68, 126
Diamond Commission · 66, 67

E
Enoch Powell · 5, 33, 34, 61, 102
Ernest Bevin · 48
European Community · 59, 62
European Research Group (ERG) · 35
European Union · 35
Exchange Rate Mechanism · 82, 89

F
Faith · 3, 17, 34, 35, 92

Fascist · 13
First World War · 11, 16, 37, 43, 113
Free Market · 1, 2, 3, 4, 20, 23, 25, 35, 42, 50, 51, 52, 53, 56, 62, 63, 66, 78, 79, 94, 97, 101, 104, 105, 106, 124, 137, 140, 142, 143, 144, 145, 146, 147
Free Trade · 33, 36, 61, 62, 64, 81, 145
Freedom · 4, 12, 19, 27, 29, 50, 67, 73, 93, 94, 95, 99, 101, 102, 105, 120, 121, 126, 130, 131, 132, 134, 140, 142, 143, 144
Friedrich Von Hayek · 1, 4, 7, 27, 61, 101, 144
Full Employment · 9, 11, 45, 46, 47, 48, 49, 50, 51, 64, 90, 92, 104, 107, 118, 119, 138

G

Gender · 32, 35
Geoffrey Howe · 82, 85, 87, 101
George Osborne · 5
Gestapo · 41
Glasnost · 19
God · 92
Great Depression · 3, 10, 13, 27, 49, 52
Grigori Rasputin · 17

H

Higher Taxes · 76, 96, 136

Housing · 31, 34, 46, 53, 54, 59, 79, 80, 84, 86, 88

I

Ideal Types · 29
Immigration · 5, 35, 56, 58, 60, 62, 142
Income Tax · 53, 60, 65, 76, 84, 87, 90, 101
Inequality · 1, 31, 63, 66, 67, 68, 69, 85, 100, 104, 139, 142, 143
Institute of Economic Affairs · 61, 101
Iron Curtain · 20

J

John Major · 77, 82, 128
John Maynard Keynes · 9, 10, 27
Joseph Stalin · 19

K

Keith Joseph · 61, 65, 101, 102, 103, 104
King's Speech · 42
Kwasi Kwarteng · 53

L

Labour Government · 37, 41, 46, 47, 65, 67, 88
Lech Walesca · 20
Leonid Brezhnev · 20
Liberalism · 5, 7, 82, 101, 135, 138, 140

M

Medium-Term Financial Strategy (MTFS) · 56, 82
Mike Tyson · 30
Mikhail Gorbachev · 19
Monetarism · 2, 4, 5, 50, 56, 61, 63, 66, 78, 81, 82, 85, 91, 94, 97, 104, 105, 127, 135, 137, 144, 145, 147
Monetary Policy · 27, 73, 82, 108, 110, 115, 116, 120, 137
Monetary Policy Committee · 28
Mrs Thatcher · 3, 4, 60, 64, 65, 66, 67, 68, 70, 71, 72, 73, 74, 77, 80, 81, 84, 88, 89, 90, 95, 100, 102, 104, 105, 116, 135, 136, 138, 140, 142, 143, 144, 147

N

National Socialism · 13
Nazi Germany · 13
Nazis · 10
New Right · 34, 50, 52, 61, 62, 63, 70, 73, 74, 77, 101, 102, 138, 139, 143, 144, 145, 146
Nigel Lawson · 82, 89, 126

O

One Nation · 31, 34, 36, 47

P

Perestroika · 19

Post-War Consensus · 47, 48, 51, 52, 56, 64, 89, 93, 105
Poverty · 1, 15, 19, 29, 31, 33, 36, 104, 139, 142
Praise · 92, 136, 140
Prime Minister · 30, 31, 35, 37, 41, 54, 59, 95, 104, 136
Privatisation · 34, 44, 84, 85, 137, 141
Public Expenditure · 44, 48, 56, 73, 79, 83, 87, 88, 96, 104, 136, 137, 141
Public Services · 42, 86

R

Railways · 17, 40, 41, 42
Red Wall · 36
Royal Commission · 39, 66
Russia · 15, 16, 17, 18, 19, 20, 130
Russian Revolution · 15, 18

S

Second World War · 47, 52, 117, 129
Seebohm Rowntree · 36, 37
Socialism · 3, 4, 12, 13, 14, 20, 71, 79, 94, 104, 129, 130, 133, 134, 135, 138, 145, 146
Soviet Union · 12, 18, 19, 20
Sybil · 31, 32, 36

T

Thatcherism · 1, 2, 3, 5, 15, 21, 48, 61, 62, 85, 92, 98, 135, 139, 140, 143, 144, 145

Trade Union · 3, 38, 44, 54, 57, 58, 60, 62, 63, 64, 66, 74, 75, 83, 84, 86, 95, 97, 125, 126, 127, 128, 137, 138

Tsar Nicholas · 16, 17, 18

U

Use of Knowledge · 21, 22, 26, 127

V

Vladimir Lenin · 18

W

Weber · 29

Welfare State · 13, 32, 33, 34, 39, 41, 46, 47, 48, 52, 67, 73, 75, 76, 92, 104, 105, 129, 131, 132, 142, 144

White Paper · 48, 54, 78, 87, 88, 91

Winston Churchill · 33, 37, 41, 42

X

Xinchou Treaty · 16